INGESTING BIG
DOSES OF LIFE

INGESTING BIG DOSES OF LIFE

TOTSIE

Library of Congress Control Number:		2020912559
ISBN:	Hardcover	978-1-9845-8697-1
	Softcover	978-1-9845-8696-4
	eBook	978-1-9845-8695-7

Print information available on the last page.

Rev. date: 07/08/2020

To order additional copies of this book, contact:
Xlibris
1-888-795-4274
www.Xlibris.com
Orders@Xlibris.com
816175

CONTENTS

INTRODUCTION

I truly believe the hardest part of any goal, journey or project is taking that first step so here goes…

There's been so much death around me lately that I have to try to make sense of it all. I haven't been sleeping good for a long time now, yet I have so much energy, almost as if I'm driven. Some people are blessed with good looks, some are blessed with good genes, and others are blessed with wealth. I was blessed with good energy. I don't know of anyone (though I'm sure you are out there) that comes close to what I'm blessed to be able to accomplish in a 24 hour period.

A conversation with my eldest son yesterday got me to thinking. We were discussing family and the recent death that seems to plague our family I know that death is part of life and I know that as surely as you live you will die. I'm just perplexed as to why some leave so early and others are left here on earth. I prefer to believe it's because there's something left here for you to do. Some mission to make this "ole" world a better place. Back to my conversation with my son. He stated, "Mom you can't save the whole world." Of course, I realize this; I didn't know that's how he perceived my efforts to help the friends and family in my world. Nevertheless, I can't miss this opportunity to reach out and try to touch someone that may have lost their way or have never been able to find it.

I believe I have a gift for gab, and I believe it should be shared. I work in the transportation department, transporting school children (for they are our future.) And it was in this occupancy that I noticed when I talked to children they actually listen and were excited to hear more.

This job gave me the opportunity to watch many small children grow and develop. Mature and come into their own individual personalities. I marvel at (and am still amazed by) the development of young minds. Somewhere along the way, I realized that when I spoke my thoughts, they were actually being heard by these children. So can I talk with you? I don't wish to talk at you, for you, or about you. I find that when I talk with someone there is always an outpouring of their own thoughts. Sooooo... LET'S TALK...

INGESTING BIG DOSES OF LIFE

As I type the date and page number, I smile because it's a blessing to wake up alive in your right mind. You see I remember being told by a woman who had suffered a nervous breakdown, that there were days when during her illness she didn't realize that there was a date, day or a measure of time. So every now and again she would announce out loud the day and the date. This assures her that her mind is still intact. The mind is such a terrible thing to waste. This holds true whether you abuse it with drugs or whether you neglect your mind for lace of use. I've had many jobs and have worn plenty hats but it's my job as a beautician and a bus driver that I think caused me to have many troubling thoughts about our world and how we have to actively seek our place in that world. As a beautician and bus driver you have to be a good listener and on many occasions give advice. Over the years I have gotten good at both.

I've heard it said that there's at least one book to be written in all of us. This book is a combination of obtained knowledge and some "deep" thoughts. My wish is that it will be able to help shorten the road to help you find "your own greatness." I KNOW. I believe that everything you go through in life, "if it doesn't kill you, it should strengthen you. Out of every catastrophe you should become stronger, out of every depression, you should become smarter. There's something to be gained from all bad situations. Every living being on this earth is SPECIAL! You have to find out what makes YOU special. What sets you aside from the crowd? It's here that a lot of us lose our way. Some never made the attempt, are never inspired enough to try. You have to DEFINE yourself. I know you heard the phrase, "you have to grow-up quick in the midst of hard times." Well you should also grow-DEEP. This would mean to not look at or think on things at surface-levels. You have to internalize your thoughts and think deep, remember your thoughts belongs to you solely, they are yours alone.

No one can enter them or take them away (unless you lose your mind, then you lose your thoughts). Having said that, begin your journey of defining yourself by exploring your thoughts, they are yours alone. I have so many thoughts going around in my head; I know this is one reason for my lack of sleep. I'm driven to write these thoughts down. I know I can't save the world, but my hope is that they will be of help to SOMEONE. What exactly describes your world? You have no say so for entering this world no say so leaving this world but you have control of all the years you spend (here) in between the two.

Identifying Your World

At the age of 16 I was on my own. I lived temporarily with a friend from school and her single mother, and several family members who included siblings and grandchildren. Ms. Jennie (that was the mother's name) had a big heart and she allowed me to stay with her in an already very cramped conditions. She went to work every day as a housekeeper and we all went to school. After school I went to a part-time job as a waitress. I helped to clean the house, cook and braid the hair of her small grandchild. I did what I could to fit in, and help out, to both not become an added burden, as well as to show appreciation for her affording me temporary shelter. The routine was the same, everyone goes to school every day and she went to work from sun up to sun down. Every Sunday Ms. Jennie would prepare the same meal: Fork hook lima beans, rice and fried pork chops, then she would spend all the remaining day in church. This was her only day off from work.

I was born in South Florida. I had two older sisters that didn't live with us. One lived with an aunt that didn't have any children and the other lived with my grandmother they were 14 and 16 years older than I and had different fathers then I did. In our home there were three children, an older sister, by two years, and a younger brother by one year. I was the middle child. My mother worked as both a housekeeper and private cook for several different families in private homes as well as big hotels on the beach in Miami.

My father was what was called a handy man. He did several kinds of jobs from landscaping to home repairs, to picking fruit. My father had no formal education and couldn't read. At age six, in Georgia he was already going to work every day to care for his mother and five younger siblings. In his later years he became bitter about his because he felt he was robbed of an education and his childhood was non-existence. He understood and appreciated the value of a good education. He went to all our parent-teacher conferences at school and was our greatest cheerleader when we got good grades. My older sister, Mary (his oldest child) was brilliant in school, Straight "A's" I was A's-B's, I didn't quite measure up. My younger brother had skills of a different sort, so Mary was Daddy's dream of escaping poverty.

My father was a man with many dreams. He came from and lived a hard life, all of his life span. Armed with his dreams, belief, hard-work (he was a hard-working man) and ambitions he was always hopeful that he could lead his family to a better life.

Soon after my sister's leaving home, my father and mother separated. My father couldn't read and what was lacking in reading skills was well made up in his ability to instill "common sense." He was a talker that was determined to get his point across to you. Before he and my mother separated he had taught his children many skills: he taught us to swim, drive a stick-shifted car, pick fruit, play card games, tell jokes, fish, study the bible, how to live a Christian life, encouraged us to dream. He never responded when someone gave him compliments on the physical looks of his children. I asked him why once, and his answer was, he wasn't concerned about our outside as much as he was our insides and he didn't want his children to become concerned with "physical looks." He processed good talking skills. It's like that saying, the blind man has good hearing, or the leg-less man has strong arms. He couldn't read but he had plenty 'common sense."

So our immediate family life consisted of my mother, my brother and me. This was at this age of 12-13 for me. We moved to a different town bout seven of eight miles away. My mother started to become sick, suffered a series of operations, then heart failure. She could no longer work. It was at the age of 13 that my step-father entered our lives. Mr. Jack as I called him was a "jack of all trades" and it was from this time until my adult life that we moved every year at least once a year, to a different town.

I went to a different school every year from seventh (7th) grade on. We had to relocate to wherever Mr. Jack could find work. He also was a hard worker.

This is how I came to be at 16 living with Ms. Jennie and my classmate and friend, Annie Pearl. My mother and step-father moved on to the next job location before the school term was over. I wanted to stay and finish the school year out before moving on the next job location. This idea of moving to different job location did one thing for me, it taught me how not to be shy. I kept meeting new and different friends every day.

As I said before I had three older sisters. The two that were 14 and 16 years older than me were professional models in Miami, Florida. They were both tall and pretty. We had the same mother but different fathers. My father was 5ft 5" short for a man; my step-father was the very same height (5ft 5"). My mother was a tall woman and I guess she had her own reasons for choosing men that were shorter in stature than her. My older sister's father was tall. Now my sister that was two years older than me (we had the same father) was very smart, straight "A" student. I was smart but not smart enough, I was an A's and B's. I also was short like my father. I was the shortest of all the children. My brother, who was one year younger than me, was the only male child in the family.

It was at a young age that I started to identify this as "my world." Earlier on I came to realize that my two older sisters were popular because of their looks, they both dated some rather famous people at one time or the other.

Now in our home, my sister Mary, who was two years older than me and very smart, had good looks and brains going for her. I always found her personality a bit odd. Smart people are often misunderstood or unable to relate to. Almost as if they're in a world of their own. It might be said that they create their own world. May be even looking at this world, as they would like it to be. My brother being the only male child gave him his special place in our siblings' world. He started out as a sickly child, over the years he became very disciplined, constant exercise, reading and studying about healthy living and eating, he became a strong and healthy young man. In fact he was the only one of us siblings that never had a weight problem. We sisters struggled with gaining and losing weight.

After Mary dropped out of school and got married so early the dimensions of my world changed. There was just my brother and me at home now so I became the oldest sibling.

It was also at this time that my mother's health worsened, she was constantly in and out of the hospital. So underwent several surgeries.

In the meantime we were still moving from town to town following whatever job location my stepfather found next. We moved up north to the state of New York. This became our last move. My mother's heath continued to fail and me and my brother shared the chores around the house. My stepfather shared the care of our mother. Mary and her family moved up too. She was still young and had four daughters by this time.

After my sister, Mary and her family moved to the State of New York I moved back to Florida to stay with my father. I guess I felt sort of sad for him; he was left in Florida alone. His three children and ex-wife were all in New York. This was my last year in school. I graduated and left to come back up North where the job situation was much better. One of my friends from Florida came back North with me, in fact to this day she's still here. Of course in later years her family also moved up North.

By this time my mother and stepfather were on the road a lot. They loved fishing and traveling. They owned a cabin in Cape Vincent (in the Thousand Islands). So I started to ponder my place in the adult world. My friend, Johnese, and I both found jobs the very first day that we went job hunting. When we arrived in New York in May 1968 the schools were still in session. Schools up North get out in June. Schools down South began in August and end in May. Up North schools open in September and end in June. This gave us an advantage over the seniors coming out into the work force here.

The first two days back in New York, we (Johnese and I) slept on the floor at my sister's apartment. We went looking and were able to find a Studio apartment. We stayed there for about two weeks until we got paid and were able to get a one-bedroom apartment. Thus began our adventure into the adult world. I loved being in control of the adult life I was entering into. I loved being able to pay my bills every week, deciding if and when and where, I wanted to go and what I wanted to do. Loved It!!! I think it's called, "Paying the cost, to be the Boss" (smile).

My brother had stayed in Florida with my father. So now in my household it was just me and Johnese. We got along well with very similar likes, dislikes, habits and we both took responsibility very seriously. We worked hard and we also partied hard.

We setup rules for our home and we both kept those rules. One week I brought the groceries, the next she brought groceries. One week I cleaned the apartment, the next week she cleaned the apartment, etc. We both went to work every day faithfully. We both paid our bills on time every week.

Okay so here I was finding my place in the adult world. In my world as a child I had to find what made me special. I didn't measure to my sister's good looks, or in the "brains" department, because I was no longer shy, I was able to develop a good personality.

"All the world's stage and the men and women are the mere actors." I started to think of this phrase every time I opened the door to leave my house. Lights, Action, roll the tape. I put on smile, adjust my attitude, on-ward and upward...

So as I entered my "adult world" I started out by simply being pleasant to co-workers and friends. My immediate goal was to be responsible and pay my bills each week.

I t was just about here at 18 that I first noticed my peers looked to me as a leader. I was given the nick-name "Mama Totsie" (Totsie being my nickname given to me by my family when I was a baby). They started asking my opinion about everything from jobs to boyfriend advice, to cooking instructions. Yes, I was a "Jack (i.e.) of all trades" and master on none. I was good at a lot of things, but my ultra-goal would be to become GREAT at filling in the blank of space between the time I came here (on earth) and the time I would have to leave. Of this I have control. I was in search of my own "greatness." I think I've always wanted this also for the people who I met and were involved with at one time or another. I think they must have felt it too, thus being the reason for asking my opinion on so many things. I was often heard saying, "If I can't help you I won't hurt you." My meaning behind this is. If I can't do something good for someone, I would never do something to purposely harm anyone.

Before I go any further in writing this book I would like to make mention that I've told just about everyone I come in contact with that I'm attempting to write a book.

I did this for several reasons. Part of it was to get or give hope that someone, anyone, could accomplish such a feat, part of it was to get thoughts or reactions from everyone around me. Since these were the people for so long that seem to think my conversations have substance, what they would think about me putting them on paper.

Years ago I wrote poetry and even got a publisher to say he would be very interested in seeing a book of poetry completed by me. A lot of my inspiration for writing poetry came from my children, over the years of me being busy with working and raising a family inspiration took a back seat to a lot of hard times and hard work. Yes, I went out that door every day thinking that the world is a stage and I was going to play my part to the hilt. It was after I became a mother and a wife that I really started to become driven.

I went from opening the door to my home every day, going out into the world with a pleasant personality and good attitude, to determination and drive. Now the thoughts that filled my head were, "good, better, best, never let them rest, until you're good is better and your better is best." I was like that commercial (~~~tries harder). Well, Totsie tries harder. In anything I did I gave 110%.

Of course in later years this stage would also end and instead of "good, better, best never let them rest until your good is better and your better is best, it became for me, WHAT IS YOUR GREATNESS!!!!! But first let me take your through my good, better, best era.

Building from Foundation

As I sat on the couch in my tiny living room I thought about my up-bringing, childhood, hardships and lessons learned.

I guess you would've considered my family as being poor, though I'm not sure we were always aware of this being the case. An immediate reminder of this was the hunger pains. Yes, there were many days we would go to school without having anything to eat. In those days you were taught never tell anyone what goes on in y our home. So we went to school hungry and hope that by the time we got home there would be at least a pot of beans on the stove. A strong sense of humor came in handy during these times. My brother would tease me as we race to the front door to see if there was any food cooking. He would say, "Look at you; you've got the white mouth." This meaning that my lips had turned white and ashy from lack of food. Then we would both burst out in laughter as we spot the pot of beans cooking on the stove. Other times my mother would say "go to school and I'll try to bring you all some lunch money.

There were lots of ups and downs in my childhood. I believe a lot of it was due to a mother who loved to gamble and a father who tried to pursue his dreams. My father knew where he wanted to go, but because he had no education he didn't have a clue as to how to get there. My mother's dreams seem to all have been about winning at "Skin" (a card game) or hitting the number, "Street-numbers." Eventually my father started playing skin and street numbers also. Thus the ups and downs and financial woes.

When they would have good luck with either the numbers or skin game there would be plenty to eat. When luck was bad there was nothing to eat. My father started out to build us a home at one point I think I was around five. We lived here for about three years. He never finished this house so we had no running water. We had to pump water from outside and used a tin tub to bath in. I can't remember having a T.V. but once for a short period before it was taken to the pawn shop and sold to buy food. Only had a phone one time when the bill doubled-up it was shut off, never got a phone again. I guess this is why I learned to play so many different card games. It was a way to entertain ourselves. And there were also a lot of singing together and telling jokes. We often made fun of our situation, a sense of humor helped. My father kept dreaming and encouraging us to dream and telling us how good life was going to be for us all someday. I eventually learned, "Nothing comes to a Sleeper but a Dream."

You have to wake-up from dreaming and put thoughts to action...

One of my father's ideas was to open up a store. That was short lived. I remember laughing at my sister who seemed to like running this store. I laughed because just about everything that a customer would ask for she would have to say "we don't have any." To me that was embarrassing. I wanted no part of running that store. Again we used humor to get through.

The store dram didn't work so next we opened up a small café. Both my mother and father were good cooks. When customer would come in and put a nickel in the juke-box daddy would encourage us to entertain them by dancing. Often times the customer would laugh and give us a quarter for the dance. Wow! This was suppose to be entertainment while the customers enjoyed their meal. What a joke!!! Again a sense of humor got us through, I smile even now thinking back on all of this.

Then there were the Cadillacs, the only car my father would buy, in fact, that became his nick-name around town. The quality and smooth ride of a Cadillac made it his only choice of a ride for a family car. Now he brought trucks for carrying his tools and lawnmowers but when the family rode, we rode in the Cadillacs.

Did I mention that these Cadillacs were always at least ten years old!! There was this grey Cadillac that every time he stopped at a red light, it wouldn't go. It had like a twenty second pause before moving. (I guess the transmission was going) this of course would make motorist behind us upset and they would blow their horns for my father to move the car. I found this both embarrassing but funny. I would slide down in my seat and hide until the car started to move. Me and my siblings would later laugh so hard our sides would hurt.

Poor daddy he had no sense of humor he never thought any of this was funny so we wouldn't let him see us laughing. I often felt his time here on earth would have been easier to bare if he had developed a "sense of humor." He was so intense. He struggled so hard, so determined, so focused, so thirsty for financial security. I only saw him relax when he had been drinking. He would tell jokes, play checkers, or card games with us or we all would sing songs. This brings me to another of his dreams.

My father and mother started a gospel singing group. There were five of them all together. The members kept changing. They would practice at our house several times a week. My father kept having us kids sing with him as he arranged and altered different songs. We all could sing a little bit but nothing earth-shaking, and certainly not worthy of fame. So, soon this dream was left behind and he started to explore other avenues. The family continued to sing together especially when we went fishing. We would sing in the car to and from our fishing trips.

I suppose my mother was the realist and she believed in my father to a point. When there was no food in the house, or no rent money, she would do what she had to do to make it happen. Often robbing Peter to pay Paul.

This would cause my parents to argue, for while she did the best she knew how to (this was all she knew) her decisions on financial survival were poorly made. I remember the "Repo" man coming to repossess one of my father's Cadillacs and my mother became very angry with the man. She wanted to physically fight the man. She actually more-or-less told the man; since I'm going to get a beating (meaning my father was going to want to fight when he finds out she hadn't made his car payments) I might as well beat you first. That man ran out of there.

Then there were the times mom would have disputes with the landlords (again because of non-payments) and school officials. My mother was quick to fight. That was her way of problem solving. I smile because I've come a very long way in life from thinking this is the answer to solving any problem. But I must include all of this as part of my beginning. This part of my Fountain. I'm very thankful for the good, the bad, the difficulties, the hard times and even the pain. For this is all a part of my road traveled and am "Thankful" for the road I traveled that has landed me here.

Everything that didn't kill me has strengthened me!!!!

My second grade teacher had a run in with my mother that she and I will never forget. I had welt marks on my back after she struck me several times for not knowing the lesson (I had been out for a week sick.) In these days you never told your parents when you got whippings. You just sucked it up. Well mom came in the bathroom while I was in the bathtub and saw the marks on my back. She went to school with me the next day and slapped my teacher so hard, she slide all the way across her desk. She told her to keep her hands off me. I was embarrassed. She left me and went home. I was never struck again but every teacher in school came at different times to stare at me while my teacher whispered, "that's the child."

My brother's head was "mauled" (a term used back in my time, when someone take their fist, balls it up and presses it against your head) by his teacher. Back to the school my mother went. She mauled the teacher's head. Then asked him, how do you like someone mauling your head? It was soon pretty well known that if my mother was at school there was going to be trouble and in the neighborhood if the landlord (or bill creditors) approached our door they were more often than not chased off.

Now a physiologist once told me and my siblings to not be alarmed that though we were raised in the same house, that we each had very differing accounts of the details that went on in that home. Meaning each child sees an event different. Each child may take a statement made and understand it to mean something different. He said this is normal of all siblings.

This story is being told from my point of view, the only view available to me. I looked back over my very young life. I had stumbled along thus far, learning from every mistake, I had a great appreciation for this long hard road. You can't tell anyone about struggles unless you, yourself have lived through them. Living through each hardship strengthened me. Every mistake made me wiser. Some mistakes I'm very ashamed of. I remember while living in Key West I told a big lie on a young lady by the name of Olatha, a lie I made up only out of jealousy I felt so bad (and still do) that this became a cure for me of being jealous. I never want that characteristic to be any part of my personality.

I have many regrets as a teenager that was part of my learning process. The ways and means I used to get "friends" of course they weren't true friends. I befriended males, trying to be their sports equal only to find out they were telling people they hung out with me because I was giving them more then I was. I hated this and it got several girls upset with me. Niokie (in Key West she could really sing) I didn't sleep with your boyfriend. And Rose in Hollywood, Florida I didn't sleep with McGee or Skoopie. It just feels good to clear the air; I hope these men and women are still alive to read this. You guys have no reason at this point in our lives not to tell the truth.

Truth be known I was a late starter when it comes to the world of boys and sex. It wasn't "cool" to be as square as I was. All the complications of relationships came later in life for me. I started working at age fifteen I was always a hard worker but the first job, I got, I lost. (I've never been fired since then). Because I gave away free hamburgers, pops, chips etc. The poor restaurant owner couldn't make a profit with me giving all the food away. This too was a way to make friends.

Had *grown to learn something about myself around this time, I really, really hated these types of mistakes, and they bothered me to the point that I never made the same mistakes twice. As I stumbled along in the learning process I liked this characteristic about myself.* I got "whippins" as a child, not very many though, and my father said I never got a whippin for the same thing twice. As he put it, I was not hard-headed. The whole building didn't have to fall on me for me to get the point.

It still baffles me to this day why some people repeatedly make the same misstates over and over, and revisits the same problems again and again. One time is the charm for me.

Still stumbling through my teenage years I would gage each hardship with what I perceived to be the hardest of times in my young life at this point that would have been the years between the ages of nine and twelve, right before we got a stepfather. There often was no food, I brought five chickens for a quarter and grew a garden in the back yard, and this helped with the food for a while. There was no money for telephones, no electricity and we took baths in tin tubs, but what I hated most, we had no T.V. At one point we lived in a house that my father began building and never finished.

Every time I went through rough spots I think back to those times and smile. I thanked God for those times, for if I can come through that I can get through this. Those time had strengthened me.

So moving forth in life I became an average teenager. Nothing in my world sets me aside as being special. I knew that my other sisters were talented and pretty. I was sandwiched between them and the only son in the family. When I found myself the eldest child living in the home, I became aware of my leadership abilities. I started hanging around a group of girls who seemed to take their clues from me. It was for that reason that I started to study myself. What were my strengths and what were my weaknesses? I knew that my parents had instilled strong survival skills, discipline, and would not put up with laziness. I can truly say none of my siblings were lazy.

Self-awareness became a new idea to my world. Everything I did up unto this point was for mere survival I my world. I realized that my parents had provided me the only skills that they processed. I likened it to watching Animal kingdom on T.V. Mama Lioness teaching their young to survive in the wilderness. You can only teach what you know. That is just another reason that I came to realize, "knowledge is power."

My survival skills were enhanced once I started my self-awareness evaluation. I was able to play to my strengths and to work on my weak points. My outlook on life at this point was fairly good, mainly because I was winning at the game of surviving. Just having a job and paying your bills was surviving.

After moving to New York and living on my own for a couple of years, I met the man I would soon wed. This was in the late 60's. Very few young girls (or boys for that matter) left the comfort of their parents' homes to live on their own at such an early age.

All the young ladies I associated with were all still living at home. Except of course my roommate, Johnese. Stepping into the adult world at an early age really matures you fast. I felt it was a good fit for me. I had a roof over my head, plenty food to eat and no bill collectors at my door. My oldest sister, Irma asked me one day how did I get the verve to move on my own. (She was 16 years older than me and had never lived on her own. If fact none of my siblings or friends lived on their own. I was always showered with questions from them all about the pros and cons of living on your own.

Life consists of a series of decisions so far I was winning at making mostly good ones, and quickly learning from the bad ones. My next role proved to be one of my "greatest."

That of a mother and wife … In this role I became "selfless"

My search for self-awareness and self-improvements were all put on hold. They were replaced instead with deep desires to rear my children with much love, knowledge, hope, devotion, and moral values. To be well rounded, to be both emotional and physically fit and to add on to that, what was given me, that is faith, and encourages them to dream and pursue those dreams. This became my biggest challenge! But definitely a labor of LOVE.

My survival mode continued as I became a wife and a mother. No time in this period of my life for self-involvement. My family came first. As I look on this period I would not have changed anything that I did as far as the time, effect, love and devotion I dedicated to my family.

I got married when I was 20 years (young) old. My husband was 21 and in the Army, this was during the Vietnam War period. William, my husband, was discharged in 1972. We began our life together; at this point we had two children. William Jr. and Robin. I worked for a bank and William was employed on the assembly line a large manufacturing company. I can definitely state that both me and my husband grew-up together right alongside of our children. We learnt as we went along. I drew from my pass experiences in my home life and of course William drew from his. While we were both raised in the South, we came from different backgrounds, therefore bringing different ideas and thoughts to the table as to how to rear our children. William was raised by a single mother, he had three sisters and one brother and he was the baby of the family. His mother worked two jobs, was very devoted to her children and her church. She often said she wished she had been able to spend more time with her children as they grew up, of course this wasn't possible since she was solely responsible for feeding, clothing and sheltering her five children. She relied on her older children to help raise the younger ones.

Everyone in this family was given chores to do; they worked together to from a strong family unit. My husband's oldest sister was 12 years older than he and he was often left in her care. In later years he looked on her as a "second mom." William considered his upbringing as being strict. He was often heard saying, "Lula Mae didn't play" (Lula being his mother's name). I came to realize that all Ms. Lula's children felt the same. They were quick to comply with her wishes. I found out later that my husband (the baby) challenged her more in his latter teen years and early adulthood than any of the rest of the children. Yes my mother-in-law was a strong presence and commanded (and deserved) a lot of respect. I admired her. She had strong Christian values and was very disciplined in her duties, paid her bills on time and I never knew her to tell a lie, kept her house very neat, taught her children those same values. All of them were neat and kept their houses clean.

My own mother passed away in 1973 from a lone and hard fought battle with heart problems. She had undergone several surgeries, had plastic valves, pacemaker and was set to have the pacemaker changed the month after she passed away. She suffered so long and often made the statement, "Lord you have let me live long enough to see my children grow-up, just take me." Remembering hearing her say this was a comfort of sort after she passed because I kept thinking now she's finally resting in peace, out of pain.

After the passing of my mother I was forced to do a different king of growing up. A lot of advice I received from Mom I had to now research and come up with answers on my own. She was now resting, how prepared was I to move forward?

About six months after my mother's passing I found that I was pregnant again. Time seem to have stood still. I couldn't remember when I had my last period. First sign was that my clothes were fitting tight. After making a doctor's appointment he couldn't tell just how far along I was. An x-ray was taken (didn't have ultra-sound back then.)

I don't remember driving home from that doctor's appointment, I am thankful I didn't hurt anyone or myself driving home. I was in a daze. When I got to my home, I remember walking in the bedroom where my husband was and telling him what the doctor had told me. I was pregnant with "twins." My mind started to immediately access my situation. The number of children we were responsible for was about to double. My mother would never know I had twins; I was a mother who was now "Motherless." I had to really dig down deep to come up with (the right) answers, wisdom, fortitude and courage to raise our children (whom I loved dearly) the best we could. I realized that being good parents carried along with it many, many responsibilities. The least of them not being instilling manners, please and thank you, excuse me, good morning, no thank you, helping to build personalities, and develop character and moral values. My children at this point and time I my life were definitely the catalyst in my life. I wanted to make sure they were well-fed, clothed, had warm shelter, were well-taught, but I also wanted them to set goals, and make plans to reach those goals. Dream, for a while, then act on those dreams. I often told them success can be measured in many ways, ask yourself what for you and your life spells success??? Then go for it.

After having my twins (both boys) life for me really changed. One of my boys was still-born. I was the mother of three children. There were plenty unanswered questions as to what happened in my pregnancy and since they never let us see or bury our child this became another painful experience in our life. A lot of questions still remain.

When I found out I was having twins, I looked into changing jobs. I felt that working at a bank didn't pay enough to afford me having to pay a babysitter for several children.

I went to school and became a cosmetologist. I was able to work opposite hours from my husband and we could work out the care of our children between the two of us. My husband had his own demons; a lot were set off because of his Vietnam experiences. He got involved with drugs. So again I took stock of my world. I was a mother of three with a husband who had a drug problem. There were a lot of problems that arises when drugs are involved. As our family went from one problem to the next I learned a valuable lesson, "Everything that doesn't kill you should make you strong."

I finished school and obtained my license to do hair. Let me tell you that working in a beauty salon is a storybook in itself. Wow!!! What characters came to the shop every week. I once said I would write a book about my experiences and adventures in the Beauty Salon. I had to cancel that idea since others have beaten me to it. There are so many books and movies about Beauty Salons.

But this is a sure place to find many, many characters. Lots of fun to be had by all too. There were many lessons to be learned here also. It was here that I learned to people watch. You found a lot of conversation in a beauty salon. A place where people (both men and women) came to relax, talk, do something for themselves, and mostly exchange ideas, thoughts (share or discuss) problems. The customers weren't just paying for a hair-do; they were paying you to be a soundboard while they talked. I became a good listener and in later years, a good advisor. Seems every possible scenario plays out at the salon. One of the first and most profound lessons I learnt was to be careful of what you say in this most public of places. You never know who knows who…I worked in this business of many, many, years and the stories are endless. I'll share a few to make you smile…. There was the time one my co-workers came to work drunk (and depressed) she tried to set her customer's hair and every time she tried to put a roller in her hair the previous roller fell out. The customer got tired of this after a while and said, "What's wrong with you?" The owner heard all of this and sent the beautician home and she finished the client. Then there was the time a beautician was working on a new client who was gossiping about her neighbor was going with a married man. For some reason the things this client was saying was familiar to the beautician so she kept pumping her for more information. This beautician lived across the street from the shop so when she put this client under the dryer she went across the street and told her husband that he was busted. She told him what she had just learned. He came back across the street with his wife and wanted to know who was in there talking his business. There was the time a drunk client got his hair done by one of my co-workers and got up from the chair and said I'm not going to pay you so what are you going to do? We all grabbed something. I grabbed scissors, another beautician grabbed a broom and the beautician he refused to pay grabbed a razor. He said okay, okay, I was just playing…And he paid her. There was the time one customer came to the shop and said she had heard that one of the beauticians had been gossiping about her. She was drunk and pulled out the longest gun I HAD EVER SEEN. Her friend took the gun (Thank God) and took her back home. The time one of the shop best customers came to the shop and told word by word, everything that was said about her the night before. Then she told us that the new client present last night was her sister-in-law, who told her everything. This doesn't include all the lies and schemes they played to get free hair-dos. One of my customers I had been doing for years got up from my chair and said, "Oh my God, I've left my pocket book at home. I never saw her from that day to this day. And finally there was the day the beautician next to me was doing her regular every two-week customer when I got a new walk-in customer. After washing my customer's hair, I turned my chair just as the beautician next to me turned hers. The two customer's feet touched each other. My customer said 'excuse me.' Her customer said, "No bitch you meant to do that." They started arguing, little did me and the other beautician know this new customer of mind had followed the wife (my new customer was the girlfriend) into the shop to start a fight. Beauty Shops have lots of DRAMA!!!! There are a lot of stories to be told from a salon. I learned to also watch each person for attitudes.

Working in a beauty salon was like participating in a 'water cooler' conversation every day. Everybody had an opinion on everything. It was interesting to me to listen to (and learn of) all the different points of views. Often giving my own opinion to what was being said. I learned over the years that it was not good to have an opinion on 'everything' so I chose my fights carefully. My best wisdom came from the older people. It was refreshing to hear wisdom being expressed so bluntly. They never tried to use big words or sophisticated phrases. That's just the way I liked it, plan and clear.

One of my co-workers at the beauty salon, Everlena and I decided to get another job to help make ends meet. She was also married and had children like me. We started to drive school buses together. We would drive the children to school, then go back to do hair in between runs. If I finished before her I would get us lunch and put hers on her bus. She would do the same for me if she finished first. We would often (about three times a week) rush home from work, cook dinner, and meet each other at bingo. We did this for about 15 years. We would say, we had two jobs, one to pay bills and the other to support our bad habits. We worked in a shop on Portland Avenue. I left the first shop after working there many, many years. The shop's owner's granddaughter was stabbed at school by another student, in a fight over a boy and died. (The family's story was told on the (Montel Williams Show.) This was a terrible, terrible tragedy!!!

The shop and the shop owner was never the same, the whole situation was too painful for me to stay there. It was so sad, so very sad. I had to leave to keep my own sanity. I left and went to another shop down the street. Six months later Everlena left also and came to the shop I worked in. We continued leaving one job and going to another together. She suddenly became very ill with blocked bowels... she was hospitalized for many weeks then went home and was out on sick leave for several more months. I doubt that she weighed 92 pounds, she was so sick and her frame was so small. After a year she got better and gained her weight back. We had broken the habit of bingo night because of her period of illness. For the next few years we both just worked and went home. She suddenly became sick again. This time she didn't make it, she died. They discovered she had Cancer. I missed her so, my work partner (and friend) had gone on....I often talked to her and said, I guess you were tired and weary, so am I but I will forge forward. After Everlena died I moved on to two other shops both also still o Portland Avenue. The last shop I worked in or will work at was Majestic Hair Design. When I left there I vowed my years of working in shops was over. My age and physical problems were catching up to me. I try to stay loyal to my old customers who had stayed loyal to me, since I specialized I old fashioned press and curl, and a lot of the beauticians today won't do them. I kept them and gave Debbie (the shop owner) most of my young customers. Debbie is a beautiful spirit, and a really good beautician. I considered myself semi-retired now. I will miss Debbie and all the wonderful customers that came to this shop. I loved the chatter, the laughter and fun of being a part of a group of such diverse people (and characters.) I even enjoyed the braggers and liars. I felt sorry for the braggers because what's so wrong with your self-esteem that you have to try to impress others with your material wealth (or your invention of wealth). It's like this…if you are watching T.V. and not on T.V.…you're one of us. Meaning, you're out here struggling like the rest of us.

I guess this is where I began to be a 'people watcher'. I love figuring them out. Don't forget I'm from the South. Northern people's attitude and living conditions are much different then where I came from. My children who were all born here (which made them one of them, Northerners). They often made comments about Southern ways. I guess my habit of speaking to people I knew from a distance bothered them most. I would see a person at the store or in the shopping mall and as soon as I saw them I would yell, 'hey, how are you?' They always thought I should wait until the person was closer and wait for them to speak to me first. When I first moved here I spoke to everyone as I approached them, or it if I was walking pass their house and they were on the porch I would speak, most never spoke back, after several years I learned not to speak. Northern people were suspicious creatures (with good cause). They felt you wanted something from them, or were up to something, or going to ask them for something if you speak to someone you didn't know. My speaking was strictly Southern matters. Same thing when I went to school here (only for one year) I addressed my teachers as yes Ma'am, no Ma'am. They told me to stop calling them that because it made them feel old. That sort of hurt my feelings because I was only doing it out of respect. Southern people are plain spoken; they say what they mean and mean what they say. I found myself looking stupid many a time with the Northern people's sarcastic remarks. They might tell you the dress you have on is pretty and at the same time be laughing at your poor choice in attire. Ole country bumpkin me. But after studying them so many years and learning their ways I fell in love with the North and I proudly called it home. I went back in my mind to my childhood and wondered how I made it out alive. I lived back in the woods in my earlier years as a child. Those woods were full of everything. We played in the woods daily. Snakes and scorpions, alligators and cock roaches, I hated cock roaches even more than snakes. My cousins lived in even more primitive conditions than we did. I spent three weeks with them one summer. They lived some two hundred miles from us. Everyday all of my cousins (two boys and two girls) would go with my aunt and uncle to pick tobacco. They thought it would be easier on me to leave me home to take care of the household chores. I had to boil the clothes in a big black pot using lye soap to clean the clothes then hang them on the clothes lines. I had to cook. I went to get vegetables and when I tried to pick some tomatoes a big black snake was wrapped around the bush. I ran back inside. I had to scrub the floors with a brush on my hands and knees. They had no indoor toilet so we had to go through the pasture to the outhouse. A large snake was wrapped around the toilet seat. I stayed constipated the whole three weeks I stayed there. Coming back through the pasture a bull charged at me (I was later told I shouldn't have put on a "red" blouse). I still have the scar on my leg as I ran for dear life and tried to get over a bob-wire fence and it stuck into my leg. I was so happy when my mother came to pick me and my brother up. Finally back home, we still dealt with things like passing worms, yes, pink worms, from your rectum what causes this I never found out. And the worms you got in your feet when you walked bare-footed in muddy water in the street, which were un-paved. You had to go in the woods and get a pine bush and burn it and put your foot over the smoke and the worm would be gone the next day. Nothing left but his skin. I don't have to contend with any of this North and I loved that. Needless to say I didn't miss those things from the South or the heat. There are many things I did miss about the South especially the beautiful beaches, the southern food, and the warm, honest, southern personalities. And I'm glad for having had those experiences for they prepared me for my future. All this was part of my foundation. It helps build a strong, a very strong foundation for me. I was not built to break. I may bend, but not break!!! I became comfortable living in the North.

So for the next 20 years I drove bus and did hair. Driving a school bus is also a whole book in itself. I will tell you more about it later on in my book. My children were growing us so fast. My house became the "Kool-Aid" kid house, meaning a lot of kids were always at my home. I would always treat them to pizza or take them to the movies along with my kids. I did a lot or preaching to the children, but I also did a lot of listening and they started asking my advice on a lot of different things.

My children came home one day and told me that in school they were asked in class to write an essay on someone you know that's not famous or family that has made a positive influence in your life. They told me over and over again my name was being read by their classmates. I smiled but made a mental note to always watch how I carried myself (or conducted myself) for others are watching. I tried to set good examples. I became everyone's "Aunt', at least people would ask are you this one or that one's Aunt? I hated to lie but didn't want to not claim these children who had clearly claimed me. I also had nieces that were around as much as possible very proudly proclaiming that they were the "real McCoy's." (blood-nieces). We did a lot of things together especially playing cards (Spades). You learn a lot of things at a card table; I guess I would catch them off their guard.

We were very involved parents; my sons and daughter were all in

Girl and Boy Scouts. I taught them all to drive and encourage them all to play sports. They were well-rounded children.

By the time I had been married about 15 years, I was forced to face a mounting problem in the face. My husband was a drug addict. I'm not talking about him for any other reason than to help someone out there who might be facing the same problem. Your "right" answer might not by my 'right" answer but this is what worked for me, and my family. I have never given anyone the advice to leave their husband, wife, girlfriend, boyfriend and I'll tell you why. First of all if they do so on your advice and see your still with your mate, they will hate you forever. They will say you told me to leave mine and you're still with yours. And secondly, when a person is truly, truly, tired and sick and tired of being tired of being "dogged" they will not only "walk" away they will "run" away and not look back. No one knows that person's breaking point but the one taking the abuse.

I can't remember at any stage in my life that I didn't assess my situation before moving forward. That is what I did now. A lot of people wanted to know why I didn't leave my husband because of his drug use. There were several reasons that I felt were good reasons for not leaving.

I think the first was my husband had been raised without a father. His father left home when he was 18 months old. He always was left with unanswered questions because of this. He said he never wanted his kids to go through this. Another reason was William; my husband never stole anything from our home. This was not in his character. H didn't steal not even with a drug habit. And third, he was always employed with a good job. It got to be routine that every week he would put bill money on my drawer every Thursday night (payday). I would get up early Friday morning and go pay bills. Every Friday afternoon before going to work William would ask I would lend him money for gas, and lunch money to go to work the following week. So it became routine that every Monday I gave him lunch and gas money for the week and every Thursday along with the bill money he would pay me back. No, we couldn't get ahead like this but we also always had shelter over our heads and food to eat. I was never lucky enough to get good paying jobs like my friends and my husband were, so I did the next best thing, I started working two jobs. I did hair and worked as breakfast shift supervisor for three years at Friendly Ice-cream, a restaurant. Then I went to school, got my license and became a realtor, I sold houses. In fact I sold myself the first home we bought. I didn't like selling houses so I looked for different types of work. I became a matron on a school bus. I did this for two years. I loved working with kids, but decided I would make a better driver then the drivers I was working with. Soooo, I trained to become a school bus driver. Anyone out there that has a dull, boring job, drive a school bus, I promise you never a dull moment. It's not for everyone and you definitely have to have your wits about you and a genuine love for children. I had both. I was able to do hair in between my school routes every day. This worked out well for me. For the first 19 years of my married life this how we worked it. Our children were all well-rounded and all got jobs when they reached 15. All three of them, first jobs were McDonalds. Our eldest son was a challenge when it came to school I wouldn't let him give-up though, it took him three years in the 12th grade to graduate. But he finally made it. He became a father young which was another reason I wouldn't let him give-up. I knew he needed an education to help pay for his child's needs. He was a good father even at his young age.

William and I became grandparents young.

Drub habits often lead to death, or jail. Well William's lead him to serving several years in jail. This was the close of another chapter in our lives. As another one opened up.

I find myself definitely in a survival mode now. I had to take care of my children and myself alone. I soon realized that my situation didn't scare me. I had been well-bred to stand firm in the face of tough times. No excuses!!! Excuses are monuments of nothing, they build bridges to nowhere. Those who use them are incompetent and are master's o nothing. Just another pretty way to say don't use excuses, as a co-worker of mine, Daniel, summed it up. I learnt that creativity doesn't flow too well when you mind is full with survival thoughts. I did get the opportunity to continue to write my poetry during this time but I did so only to keep myself inspired to continue to keep putting one foot down in front of the other. I've always had a fear of "falling down." I think if I should fall I will never get us again. Falling by the wayside, getting stepped on by the strong, as they continue on their pass to success, never to stand again. I shall never fall, I pledge that to myself. I may give-out but I will never give-up. I keep putting one foot down in front of the other. It was during this time that I wrote one of my many poems to remind myself its (live life) durable.

TAIN'T

Hey, taint no reason not to try your best
Taint no reason to settle for less
Tis your duty to work hard and strive,
And by your rewards stand tall.

Tis your right to have these things,
Taint nothing to it at all.

I had (have) several different things I *did (do) every morning to set my mood. Call them rituals, if you must. It starts with Thanksgiving the Lord for waking-up alive, pain-free and in my right mind. Thanking Him for having a home to wake-up in and for a bed to get out of, for clothes to put on, for food to eat, for a car to drive to work in (or a bus to take me there) for having job(s) to got to etc., etc., etc..... So that by the time I get to work I'm in a very grateful mood.* Right before I go in the building I recite Shakespeare, *"This assures me that my attitude has been properly adjusted. All the world is a stage and the men and women are the mere actors/actresses." So I am on stage, as I enter the workplace. Lights, camera, action, I'm bound and determined to put on the performance of a life time. Whether I felt like crying or not I always would put a big smile on my face and start to perform. I was only able to calm down and be myself when I unlocked the front door to my home, and went inside after work. If I had to cry that was the time...I had pulled it off once more.*

This is how I got through each day and because I was a private person, I felt no one at work was responsible for my problems, nor could they help me solve them. I shouldn't impose my problems on them. Later on in years I came to find out that I was being watched and admired for the way I handled myself during these hard times.

I went to visit my husband every other week taking him boxes of food and money. I drove the 110 mile trip, mostly alone. Sometimes maybe my three children went to see their father with me and an inmate there girlfriend rode with me a few times. William had a couple of friends that went with me a couple of times. My sister went with me the first time to help me find my way. I got settled into this routine. I was still working both jobs, doing hair and driving school bus. I had promised William I would keep the home-fires burning until his return. We had been married 18 years when he went in. Our children were growing up as were the children I drove back and forth to school everyday I continue to people-watch on my school bus the same way I people watched at the beauty salon. I found it amazing to watch these little people grow up as well as develop well-rounded personalities. Each different and unique.

You can't fool children, they can tell whether you're there for the pay check or if you really care about them. I choose to pick my fights. I believe you have to allow as much for ducking as you do dodging. In other words you can't get on them for every little thing they did. My main concern was making it a safe ride. I was satisfied if they remain seated, kept their hands to themselves, and kept the noise level down so I could hear as well as see any danger. I did this for over 23 years and it was very rewarding to have my students come back to me after they were grown to tell me something I said or did made a difference in their lives, very rewarding indeed…I coined this phrase on the bus, Ghetto-ism. I explain what Ghetto-ism means; it's participating in destructive behavior, and allowing yourself to live in dirty conditions. I would watch one child throw paper across the buss to another child and the paper lands on the floor. I would tell that child that there's no throwing paper o this bus and no Ghetto-ism to so pick up the paper and place it in the garbage can. If I catch them writing on my seats or cutting the seats, I would tell the whole bus that Joey or Mary is practicing Ghetto-ism. No one wanted to acknowledge that they were in any way a part of the Ghetto whether they came from there or not. When they would walk pass a piece of paper on the floor or on your lawn is Ghetto-ism). They soon caught on quick, and if anyone would see anyone else walking pass paper on the floor or throwing paper or writing on the seats they would yell out loud that this person is practicing Ghetto-ism. I got really good at having reasonable conversations with parents too. This came in handy later on as my position in the company changed. I was always fair, but firm with my students. If you play with a puppy he will lick you in the mouth. In other words you get too playful with them; they will play too much with you. I kept busy working and set into this routine. I received many Blessings as I fought to keep everything together. I was very thankful. Some Blessings the Lord sent, but the Devil brought them too...simply put, the Good Lord was looking out for me in spite of everything.

Hard times.

Everyone has cycles, or periods where life is good, blessed, plentiful and then there's the times where you don't know where your shelter or food will come from tomorrow. I shouldn't say everyone, let's just say most. Some people are born with it, live with it, and die (though they can't take it with them) having it, money that is. The rest of us had to as they say, "roll with the punches."

I took these punches as a foundation, to me it meant that as I got through each rough spot and came out on the other side still alive and kicking, I grew. I grew stronger and wiser. If faced with the same situation again, I knew I could handle it. I knew I could get through it. Everything that doesn't kill you makes you strong (or should).

There were plenty enough rough spots (hard-times) to go around. There was a client of mine that walked five miles, she was seven months pregnant, to borrow a dollar to get her children (seven of them) some spaghetti sauce. This enabled her to make a large pot of spaghetti and sauce and didn't include any meat. It fed her children for one more day. Shut-offs for Gas and Electric were everywhere in the community and it wasn't unusual to see extension cords running from one house to another to allow ones neighbor limited electricity. I had a neighbor on the evening news one day that got arrested because she refuses to leave Social Services without food stamps or money. She threw herself across the desk and wouldn't let go. She said she wasn't going to go home and look into the eyes of her hungry children without bringing them something to eat. Every first of the month you saw people moving in and out of apartments for non-payment of rent. Some moving on to other apartments, some getting all their belongings tossed on the curb.

Those fortunate enough to have somewhere to move to would be all grins for another month. These people had hope (and or Faith). Often times keeping their Faith in tact by going to church listening to the "word" and either saying, Amen or "Ouch." This was the group of churchgoers that weren't very dutiful in church. They went to simply try to gather strength (or favor) in church if what was being taught stepped on their toes, they said, "ouch." If they were a witness to the word they said, Amen.

It wasn't hard to understand why churches and communities weren't able to get very many volunteers in poor areas. Poor people have very little time or space in their heads to commit to anything but how to get and keep shelter over their heads, food in their mouth, and to pay their bills, period! In other words, middle class people go to the grocery store and the clerk asks, would you like to donate to 'feed a family" today? The quick response from the poor would be, "Let me feed this family first." Pay for their grocery and leave.

Those were the hard times I was faced with as an adult. I began to understand why my father was so tensed and stressed as a parent. I had three mouths depending on me for shelter and food, looking up to me to do and say the "right things." Asking my advice on everything and watching, I mean really watching me to see if I would live up to their expectations and I was aware that those expectations were set high. I could not afford to disappoint them. This being my greatest challenge thus far I life, I had to rise to the occasion. As a natural progression of things as I got older, I grew wiser. William and

I were young parents but we all grew-up together and I hoped that as our kids grew up that along with age will also come wisdom. The older I got the more I appreciated the flow of knowledge coming my way and I was very glad to use it. I started to realize that as you grow older and lose your youthful looks and shape you are compensated by what you loose on the outside with a different kind of beauty on the inside. It's up to you to expose that inner beauty to those you meet. The wonderful thing about inner beauty is it doesn't fade away and is capable to growing and glowing. I would never, ever want to exchange my knowledge (and age) for youth. No way!! However, if it was possible to have both I would gladly accept and there would be a lot less mistakes made as I stumbled through life.

I have to admit I didn't have the struggles that my parents had to endure, and my children always had food and were well-dressed. I wasn't one to care about spending my money on name-brand clothes but I soon realized that the children now-a-day were under a lot of pressure to dress the status-quo. I was continually, always blessed to have two jobs. I was never without work. Thank You Lord! Still my parents had so much more to contend with trying to raise their children. When I was four I was sleeping and was awaken by my mother pulling me out of the bottom of the bed by my foot. There was a large snake coming down the wall at the head of the bed. I remember when I was seven there were suddenly a swarm of flying cock-roaches that came out of nowhere and my sister turned the light on and they were all over that white sheet. I had none of these things to threaten my children's safety up North. My parents were unable to get and keep continual jobs. That made a huge difference. Still these were hard times, my two jobs made the difference for me and my children. A poem I started to write comes to mind...

The Fallen Man

The fallen man we see each day.
In dirty streets and alleys he lay.
The man that life has robbed of self-respect.
We must take it for granted that he's done his best.
For who are we to say he wasn't once able and strong.
We know not of his good deeds nor of his wrong.

Well we made it through and it was time for William to come home.

By the time, William got out he and I had been married 20 years. Our kids were almost grown and almost out of the house. My daughter was in college and had become a young mother herself. She and her daughter would continue to live with us until she finished school. She then worked for two years working two jobs, and left home to move in her own apartment. All our children had jobs at this point. Williams and I could move forward with different goals. I am thankful for the help I received from friends and family members who all helped during the years of Williams's drug abuse. William's sister Jessie had no children of her own and played Santa every year for all the children in the family. She seemed to love spending hundreds and hundreds of dollars on them year after year. I was very mindful that no one has to do anything for you and that you should show your appreciation when they do. Jessie loved little girls and when my daughter started school, she bought her 17 new outfits!!!! I was always truly grateful for everyone's help. Williams's oldest sister, Tina, was a big help also. They never turned us down for favors. I won't forget the help over the years of my many, many friends, many them dead now. Yeedrah, Birder and Charlene, we have traded favors and borrowed money back and forth for years. They can still get anything I have, and I believe they feel the same about me. Yes, it's been said that by the time you are 50 half the people you know will have died. And as I go over in my mind all my deceased friends and family, this saying cannot be more truthful. My sister and brother were plenty help also but my mother-in-law helped both financially and inspirationally. We had stuck it out together and better days were ahead.

William stayed drug-free and started to see life in a different light. He joined the church and decided he wanted to go back to school. He was very appreciative of the education he didn't get the first time around. He worked very hard on trying to stay focused on his schoolwork. This was not easy for him after years of drug abuse there's a certain part of your brain that the drugs have killed off. Remember, a mind is a terrible thing to waste. He wanted this so badly! I helped him all I could and finally he graduated from college with a degree in Auto mechanics. He was able to work on cars with computer engines. I was so proud of him as were his mother and children; we were all screams at his graduation. William now had a thirst for living life to the fullest. He wanted to find and get to know all his family members but most of all he wanted to travel back to Mississippi every year to care for his brother who suffered with muscular dystrophy. For the next 10 years, straight we traveled to Mississippi to help his brother, Eddie. Often we all travelled together three carloads. William enjoyed taking his brother out of the house to sight see, or for doctor's visits (he had to physically carry him to the car) oftentimes he (Eddie) would cry out in pain when he moved him and Williams loved doing repairs around the house. Eddie's sisters enjoyed buying him anything he had a taste for to eat and me, I enjoyed cooking weeks' worth of his favorite foods to leave there for him after we were gone. I always wanted to be the first to leave coming back up North. It was hard for me to see the sadness in Eddie's yes when we all had to say good-bye each year. We always left him smiling because the others were still there.

Now this was a new and different era in my life, our children had grown up and were all finding their own way. William was drug free and loved spending time with his grandchildren. I was both relieved and happy that our children had reached adulthood while William and I were still alive. I use to ponder in my mind who I would want to finish raising our children in case of death. I always knew the answer would be no one. Not that we both didn't have good and decent relatives on both sides but to me no one was a perfect fit. I'm so thankful I never had to choose. As I look at our oldest child, his passion for music made it easy to predict his future. From the time, this child was 11 months his father would tell him to crawl over to the stereo and put on a certain record. He would do it and I couldn't figure out how he knew which record to choose since at 11 months he couldn't read. He would then bounce around on the floor dancing to the music. His father and I loved this!! Couldn't even walk (all my children walked late because they were so over-weight, all three of them weighed 30 pounds at nine months) but he bounced up and down on the floor. He enjoyed music, as did his dad. So it was no surprise that he grew up to be a "DJ." My daughter grew up to be never without a plan; she planned and prepared for everything. She was and is very private and independent. She's a better woman than me in the sense that she would do without before asking a favor. One day I know this will change, no man is an island. She earned and received her degree in the field of Criminal Justice. Our third child could never connect and I'm sure it's because the person he wanted to be connected to wasn't here, his twin brother. They were grown and the baton seemed to have been passed. I told my children that I have to push them farther then I went I school and that they had to push their children further than they went in school. All my children had some college education.

William and I traveled a lot at this time, seems he now had a thirst for finding and getting to know "family." For some 10 years, straight we went to Mississippi to visit and to take care of his brother. He would also seek and find old friends and told me over and over stories about things that happened in his childhood.

Those trips became our getaway every year but life went on with us both working, paying bills and saving for our yearly vacation.

We had grown up so much and so had our children. So now, I begin a new journey on lessons learned from the beauty shop and the school bus. I enjoyed both jobs and became educated (in a different way) from them.

I always felt blessed to have two jobs. It's not often that you can be gainfully employed without any layoffs and to enjoy what you do on both jobs. I was fully aware that no one was going to just give me anything and if I had to earn it, I was blessed with doing something I enjoyed. Hard times were still around and I watched with horror and saw some horrible things come to past. As I continued to drive bus, I realized these children nowadays were living in terrible conditions. Listening to the transmissions on the bus radio left no doubt of this. One day a driver called in to say he was at a particular address to pick up a child and the child ran out crying with his pants in his hands stating his uncle had just raped him. The driver was calling saying, get the police here. Another driver called in another time and said as he pulled up to the address the student ran out with his brother in his arms, dressed in a diaper only. The student stated a man was inside beating his mother. It was later found out that the mother was on drugs and the drug dealer was beating her because she had not paid him for his drugs. These children were definitely 'cut from a different cloth' than those of former years. I truly believe these kids were coming from drug addicts' homes and being raised by parents who were kids themselves. And we all heard about the babies that were born to "crack addicts" well I think these children are "crack babies growing up." They have no conscious, no regard for human life, no self-respect, therefore cannot respect anyone else and no parent to teach or instill any values in them. I was on a bus helping this driver get through his route (I was being a matron) when he got to this child's house, he said 'go in and get your father'; I want to talk to him about your behavior. This child told that driver, 'he's not my father, he just fucks my mother and pays the bills...wow!!!!! What a statement to come out of a child's mouth. I can give you many, many more examples and proof of why I say these children need help. I looked on each and every one of them with pity and wondered where I could make a difference because bottom line, THEY DIDN'T ASK TO BE BORN!!! Where were these people who brought them into this world and felt the responsibility ended there?

There were plenty enough problems to be had by my clients in the beauty shop too. The difference were these were grown-ups, with problems they felt there were no answers to. Several people I knew committed suicide. Oh if only they had waited another day to see their better tomorrow. You have to live through it, go around it, under it, and get over it but don't give up. Keep putting down one foot, over the other. You cannot leave that kind of legacy for your children. If your children see you give up they will think, 'if Mom or Dad couldn't do it I can't either, but if they see you stumble through it and make it they know it can be done. You cannot stop putting one foot down in front of the other. You have to live through the bad to get to the good. The good is always around the corner. You just have to keep turning corners until you get there. God and bad times comes in cycles. When you're in a good cycle, rest, until the bad comes again and when you're in a bad cycle stand tough until the good comes again.

I want to stop here and repeat these facts about my life are as I see them. Anyone mentioned in this book that has a different 'take' on anything I said feel free to write your own book. In fact, I encourage you to do just that, I wish that my nephews would follow my examples and find themselves a project that could bring them to the peak of their own greatness. I'll be the first to validate their pain but what comes out of the pain is strictly up to you. Are you listening Darryl, Darc, Stanley, Corey, Craig. Cameron you are already set at solving your issues I see you used your pain to motivate you to find ways to understand yourself and the world you were born into, since you have your own book published "Empty Buckets."

I feel that since I'm a real person to all of you that you will realize that all you have to do is be determined, get a skill, set goals, and believe in yourselves. Don't give up!!! Success could be around the next corner. Keep putting down one foot in front of the other.

William, my husband, had become driven with his newfound life as a drug-free man. He wanted to experience and do everything. It was as if he had found out how much fun it could be to live in the land of the living. He wanted to try everything.

He would fish, hunt (one of his friends shot him the buttocks, mistaking him for a deer) and he loved to ride on his motorcycle with his friends. I'll never forget the day the hospital called me and told me he was in the trauma unit after having an accident on his cycle. They had put stitches in both his legs by the time I got there. One leg was so big it looked like it had a small head attached to it. As soon as they finished examining him, he wanted to go back and get his motorcycle. Wow! It didn't faze him one bit that he was just involved in an accident. I took him home where he immediately called a friend to take him back to pick up the motorcycle.

My father past on during this period. He died in a nursing home in 2003. We took comfort in the fact that he kept saying, I die a happy man, I've been treated like a 'king' my sister would visit him one day and me the next. In fact, some of the residents didn't know that we were two different people. A lot of people think we look that much alike. William loved daddy, and daddy loved William. Williams went back to riding his motorcycle. I had this strange feeling about the cycle but couldn't stop him from riding. I expressed my feelings to his sisters and mother. This is what he wanted to do!!!!!

In my world people didn't have a lot of skills or money or plans. Instead they relied on 'luck' and dreams. If they had sport skills they were one up on the next man. I taught my children that they have to set goals, plan and work hard to accomplish anything they desire. Playing cards, bingo, the horses and lotto were just some of the ways we hoped to become rich. Have your ever notice that when the 'big' break came and they were blessed with a large sum of money that most of them had no idea of how to turn that money over or to spend it wisely. They simply keep spending it until it's all gone. Sharing is fine, but when you share never tell the friend or family member the total amount you were blessed with. I'll tell you why I say this. If you won five million on the lottery and you gave your sister $5,000. She will only think about the amount you had left after sharing with her and why couldn't you give her more. Everybody can find a way to spend your money better than you can. But if you had just given them the money they won't have an amount in their head that they want to help you finish spending. Another reason is when you're broke that amount forever sticks in your mind. They want to know what in the world you spent five million dollars on. You hit the lottery or the horses is best, believe me, to not give the amount of your winnings. We get a large amount of money from Income Taxes and we know only to pay up bills (not that we shouldn't) but we have no idea how to turn-over money to make more money. Dreaming and wishing our lives away. Nothing comes to a sleeper but a dream.' We have to trade our 'wish bones', for back bone!!!

I have come to realize that some people don't have the drive, will power, ambition and determination required to find their own success. Somewhere along the line they didn't receive the support, encouragement and guidance to help them achieve their own personal successes. We are moving into the age of computers. What happen to "Mama Say" short or long talks with grandparents. It's like young people no longer wanted to hear of their history. Almost as if it hurts too much to hear it. People of my age wanted them to know how far they have come but the young people only questioned why we were so far behind in the first place. They have no desire to look back into the darkness. I loved listening to senior citizens but my young people felt all their answers should come from computers. Computers have plenty knowledge but you can't get wisdom from a computer!!!

And what about plain ole "common sense." Can we figure out anything without asking the computer???? Will the use of the good ole brain get to be outdated???

One thing is for sure answers come from the computers are not tempered with love, patience, and a personal touch to make sure the answer 'rings a bell' in the head of the intended.

A lot is loss by asking a machine to tell you 'basic' answers. Nevertheless a correct answer.

Now our children were grown and gone. I stopped to ponder

what this meant at this stage of our life. I figured it should be down hill from here. I went back in my mind. Just how much did we stumble before we reared these three adults. There were struggles along the way, and what perceptions did these three come away with?

How did they feel about their 'family structure.' I know some of the things I did to make it was embarrassing to them. I would pull our little red a wagon full of dirty clothes. Then there was the time in the middle of a snowstorm I couldn't get a taxi so I put the grocery (all ten bags) on the bus and got off at the stop two blocks from my house. I had to stay there until I saw someone come by that knew me or my children. Finally one of my son's friend walked by. I had him to take two bags and to knock on my door and to tell them I'm at the bus stop waiting with eight bags of grocery.

These of course were the days before cell phones. We were without electricity a few times, also I think the lights got turned off a total of three times but never more than a day. "Piece of cake", especially since as a child the lights were off a lot.

I have my hang-ups from childhood and I wanted to make sure my children didn't come away from their childhood with the baggage I did. Not having a T.V. for several years and going to bed hungry still bothers me today. That's why every Saturday I have steak (porterhouse) baked potatoes and salad. Couldn't afford steak back then. And I have a T.V. in every room, over-doing it I know. It use to bother me to hear my children say, "I'm hungry." They only meant that they were ready to eat. But I would tell them to say you're ready to eat because, Thank God! You have never gone hungry. To be hungry means you went without food for days, not hours.

I remember trying to get to work and my car wouldn't start so I walked to Main Street to catch a bus to take my children to the babysitter. The snow really started to come down hard. I had a baby in my arms and my son who's hand I was holding suddenly started to cry and didn't want to walk, his feet had become cold. I had to pick him us as well. I was carrying two babies, a diaper bag and a pocket book. I tried to flag down a taxi once I reached Main Street. I waved and he waved back smiling and kept going. I could have cried but I know if I did my children would start to cry also. My situation seemed hopeless. All of a sudden a Transit bus driver on his way back to the barn with his bus pulled over got out of the bus grabbed one of my children and put us on his bus and drove us home right up to my door (Lord I was grateful, especially since I know he could have lost his job for doing this). He said, 'go inside and stay, you shouldn't be out here in this weather with these children.

I can't describe how I felt that day being stuck in a storm with my children but I can tell you one thing, from that day to this, I promised myself, I would never, never pass a mother with the children walking in a storm. I forever feel that pain. I've kept my promise. If I'm blessed to be riding I won't pass a mother (or father) with children walking in a storm.

I felt my struggles were no harder or different from others in my world. Nothing earth-shaking, nothing that I couldn't deal with. Everything that I had gone through in my childhood and as an adult was my cushion of strength. Every time I went back in my mind to those times I would smile because I knew these were the things that had strengthen me. I had become a strong woman. I began to realize this too when it came to dealing with not only my children but the children on my bus. I can say this now and realize I dodged a many bullets. I wasn't a strict parent and I wasn't a strict bus driver. I was firm but fair. A child knows your heart, they can tell whether you are there for a pay check or whether you really care about them. My own children could tell when I meant what I said. I wouldn't let my children make a lie out of me when I said I would do this or that for punishment if they didn't correct their behavior I would do just what I promised I would. I allowed as much for "ducking as I did for dodging" simply put, I might say no to one thing but yeas to another. I never said 'no' to my children without giving them the reason why. I never allowed my children to spend the night at friends houses but I would allow friends to stay at our house. You see I knew what went on at my house but I didn't know what went on in anyone else's house. There were rules to riding the school bus. The rules were in the front of the bus on a sign. I choose the three most important ones (for me) and wouldn't say too much if they didn't follow the others. I realized thye had been confined all day to a classroom and needed a little freedom. The three rules that mattered most to me were: (1) stay in your seat; (2) keep the noise level down (I needed to see as well as hear my approaching danger) (3) keep your hands to yourself, not hitting other children.

Now I'm a woman of small statue. I'm only 5ft. My voice is my biggest weapon. It's very strong, forceful, deep and loud. I use it to my advantage. It's very commanding when I'm upset and very endearing when I wish to be charming. Now my own children all said after they grew up (they were all in their 30's when they said this) they never knew I was short. They never paid attention to my height, it was always about what I said and how I was saying it. They said,'and to think we were so afraid of a woman so small.' I had several tricks that worked for me on my bus as well. I never got out of my seat to stand toe to toe with a child (they would quickly see they towered over me and when I went back to talk to a child who was seated I never got close without wearing expensive cologne. Now I've just revealed one of my closet secrets (I have many more.) My reasoning for the cologne is this. Smelling good made them less defensive and appealing to their senses, made them more responsive to what you're trying to teach them. Another way of getting my children on the bus to listen was to show them that each and everyone of them were special to the world and I wanted them to come to know that for themselves, so every morning I would have something different to say to each child that would pertain to why that child is special. This formed the basic for a relationship with each child. I did this with my own children also, because they were each special to me. I had three children. I told my oldest (a son). This he was my special child because he was my first born, (and he is) and I told my daughter she is special to me because she is my only daughter (and she is) and I told my youngest son he is special to me because he is my baby (and he is). Every child (for that matter, everyone) wants and needs to feel special.

Now my children are all grown and gone. I began to look for ways to fill the void in my life. I still had plenty energy so I worked my two jobs. Those two jobs and a husband should have been enough to keep me occupied. But it wasn't.

I often told people I knew that if they were bored to drive a school bus. I can absolutely without a doubt tell you its' impossible to be bored driving a bus. From the time I stepped into the bus terminal to the time I got back into my car to drive home it was both a complex and interesting job. All the characters were not only found on the bus but also in the bus terminal. It takes a special kind of person to drive school bus and some of these people were unique, smart, odd and looking for something different. And they found it when they started driving a school bus. Somewere well-off and retired but didn't want to stay home with their retired wives or husbands and be ontheir spouses "Honey-Do" list. Honey do this or honey do that. My co-workers were from all walks of life and even different countries. We all shared a common goal, picking the children up and dropping them off safely every day. Everything in between getting the job done became very interesting. Just listening to the radio transmissions between dispatchers and the buses would give most of us conversation to take to the dinner table. You could very easily determine those drivers that would not last a month, just by the questions they asked over the radio. And the there were those who got on the air and come unglued with a situation on their bus, or with something they are witnessing on the street. Calls would come in saying such things as 'there's a fight between two motorist here on Monroe Avenue, then he proceeded to give the blow-by-blow account of the fight. Or a driver turns down Conkey Avenue and almost hit a lady who runs in the street stalk-naked!!!

Then there's the end-less fights reported between girlfriends and boyfriends out in the streets. Even have reports of angry parents jumping on buses attacking the driver or even other students whom they claim are bothering their child. (this sort of thing only caused a situation to snow-ball. Because the next day the parent of the child that was attacked will want to get on and attack that child who's mother attacked her child. That's why you are not to open the door when you see angry parent at a stop. You talk to them from the window only. So much violence!! And violence is definitely not the answer!! It is during this period that I became very good at 'problem solving' between child, parents, or bus driver and parent. I find that 90% of the problem is a lack of communication, or mis-communication. Understanding is a beautiful thing!!!!

The dispatcher at my job busted his knee and was out of work for several weeks. One exceptional busy day I went into the office to ask a question and saw the phones ringing and the manager was trying to answer the phones and dispatch the radio and was getting overwhelmed. I started helping and the rest is history. They asked me to start dispatching. I had driven bus for 13 years, I now became the dispatcher, without any formal training. I felt that dispatching was a common sense job. You basically helped each person to solve whatever problem they were facing, whether it was permission to turn right on red, or a child locked out or needing to back up with assistance (never back a bus without assistance) or call a trouble-shooter to the bus for a fight. Or in emergencies call an ambulance for a sick child.

I loved my job as a dispatcher. It was just as fulfilling as driving the school bus, may be not rewarding because I loved seeing the little children change and grow each year as they developed both mentally and physically. You actually get to see the personalities of each of them form. I was still doing my part to see them get to school every day;. I was a 'dinosaur' of sorts. I came to work every day. My dedication was unmatched. I would get excuses from the drivers, such as I have to go with my daughter to take her dog to the vet, or I have to help a friend move, or I have to get my nails done. I couldn't believe that a job that only requires you to be here 180 days out of 365 days a year would have so many absentees a week. I just felt there was no dedication to getting the children to and form school. Don't get me wrong there were several drivers like myself that never missed a day. But only a hand full. If we got a really sunny day they would call in, if they got their income tax return back they would call in. if they hit bingo the night before, they called in and if they hit the lotto, they are out until the money is spent. I didn't make much sense to me because once the money is spent, you are broke and they wouldn't even have a paycheck at the end of the week because they hadn't worked all week. Wow!!! That's just crazy, which is why some of them didn't have a 'bucket of piss or a window to throw it out of'. I really knew my time was coming to an end when a different company took over. Their concerns were less about dedicated employees and more about computer experienced people. They were there to make the big bucks, forget about the caring and sharing of the community, they didn't even live in the country, let alone the community. Oh well, that's the way business ventures go. I still wanted to see our children get the education they so badly needed. **THEY ARE OUR FUTURE!!!!**

Once again I have to face the fact that computers were taking over. I must admit here and now that is one of the reasons for me trying to empty my thoughts, knowledge and wisdom out of my head before losing it. I've lived long enough to see a lot of wise people crumble to where their thoughts are no more. We are mere humans. We can't seem to sustain our 'data' as we age. I'm choosing to empty my mind as much as I can. This became a pivotal point in my career, I was losing to computers.

It was during this time that my father passed away in a nursing home. He lost his battle with fighting to keep his mind. Not an educated man but a 'wise' man. I am a 'sandwich' generation, I took care of my parents and my grandchildren. I can rest easy with that thought. I should say, 'we' took care of our parents because my siblings did their share. We can be proud of that fact.

It's funny but after my father died I began to pay closer attention to the older parents here from the "south." They were all being taken care by their children. They seem to all have one thing the common, 'Po-Mouthing'!! What is meant by this is simply, I don't care how well-cared for these parents were, they seem to think they had to beg for more from anyone that will listen, which embarrassed their children. To their way for thinking, getting something 'extra' to hide or put away would keep them prepared for any emergency, it's their survival skills 'kicking-in."

My father's passing had been a long slow road of deterioration. He had dementia. When we first noticed a change in his mental state it was actually cute even, funny but this turned serious near his end. The man that had given us so much wisdom had disappeared into this confused, lonely man. He seemed locked in a world of his own, where we could no longer reach him. There were times when he would bring up something that happened 35 or 40 years before but could not remember what day it was or whether he had any visitors that day. The loss of your brain certainly brings down your quality of life. That very thought had me wondering how we can preserve our thoughts and memories.

At the bus terminal every day as I dispatched, the drivers would come in and get coffee while they warmed their buses up. The daily conversation went from the sports game the night before, to political subjects, religion, the cost of living, it ran the whole gambit. Some seem to have an opinion about everything, some never had an opinion of anything. Some chose to speak only on things they knew well. I was once told that an opinion is just like an 'ass-hole' everyone has one. As I listen in between my duties to these drivers talking every day, some seem to empty out their mind daily. Good, bad, or indifference, they were determined to give you their thoughts on everything! I find that usually these are the people that are lonely, the people that have talkative spouse, mother, father, etc., seem to be quiet. Those that emptied their thoughts out every day didn't much interest me. I knew what they were thinking because they had no problem telling you. It's the ones that came in and never engaged in the conversation that interested me most.

That song passed through my mind, how does is go…'nobody knows what goes on in my mind but me'. So true!!! If you don't state your mind, no one can read your mind. Some are so willing to tell all and others aren't willing to tell anything. I have learned to pay attention to the ones that aren't willing to open up. I was good at telling you the mood or attitude of a person entering the room, but I couldn't recall what that person was wearing. I never looked at the 'outside' I was always seeking a view of the inside. I can scan a room and tell you who will most likely go off firs. I don't care about the pretty dress you are wearing or the tight jeans that hug your hips. I want to look into your eyes (The mirror to your soul) and see who's in there!!

I believe that a doctors job is to know medicine. Your job is to know your own body, pay attention to the changes and to the reaction to certain foods, you can be of much help in adjustments in your own regiments. And so I watched, looked and listened and realized that the mind is really a terrible thing to waste!!! Good physical and mental health is such a Blessing, you can be in good health one minute and down the next!!! I see so much evidence of this. It's like, Whoops, there it is…All of a sudden. Well that's the way life hit me on the home front. I had to fight to keep my mind. I think if it wasn't for so many people telling me they admired the way I carried myself I would have fell short. I couldn't afford to do that with so many people watching the outcome. Watching my example!!!!

Now speaking of health, my husband's health seem to take a turn for the worse. You would think since he had stop taking drugs and smoking his health would flourish, not the case. First he had a by-pass on his leg. This did not go well and they had to take him back to surgery three hours after leaving there. The by-pass never healed properly and infection set in. They did skin grafts and the skin continually rolled back away from the area. He came home from the hospital but lived in the living room in a hospital bed with a bed-pan. A nurse came out twice a day to clean and change his bandages. He stayed in that bed for six months. They finally put him back in the hospital to remove the plastic tubing they had put in his leg. They put him in insolation because they said his leg was so full of infection. No one came to his room for three days. They all kept making excuses as to what would happen next and who would perform it. It was crazy!!! I went to the hospital administration office and demanded someone do something, finally they sent a specialist from another hospital to remove the plastic tubing they had placed in his leg. At this point he had lost 45 lbs. (he was already a small man he was 5'11 and weighed 140 lbs.) After this was done they couldn't say whether he would lose that leg or not, they said they didn't have enough history on this sort of thing to know what the future held for him. He now had one leg much smaller than the other. He went through months, and months of therapy. During this year and a half of operations and therapy I was afraid that he would get hooked on pain pills. After getting through his of deal, and getting back on his feet he ad a renewed appreciation of life and being able to do the simple things. We traveled every year for the next 10 years to Mississippi to help care for his brother who had muscular dystrophy. Being drug free and pain free seemed to make William determined to experience new and different adventures. He wasn't afraid to try anything and the same held true for food he wanted to taste and try anything that he had never tried before.

He joined the church. He went on fishing trips for the weekend. He hunted and caught several deer. He learned to make chili with deer meat, he learned to cook tripe. He made soups and sauces. He became a good cook. And finally he fell in love with motorcycles. He brought a cycle and joined a motorcycle club. He drove his cycle whenever the weather would permit. He got hit twice, once on the way to work and once on the way from work. This didn't stop him he would get stitched-up and would get right back on that motorcycle. He kept using the excuse that he could ride all day on two dollars worth of gas. (The price of gasoline was very high).

He went out riding one night (a Wednesday night) with his motorcycle friends and got into another accident. This was in August, we would celebrate 35 years of marriage in September.

As he turned the corner the rider on the motorcycle behind him, front wheel hit his back wheel and they both were thrown into a tree. William's skull was crushed and he died on the spot!!!

My life would never, never be the same again. My husband was dead. It hurt to breath, I had to force myself to take air in and out of my lungs. In between the tears and the gut wrenching sobs I realized I had to plan my husband's going home celebration. All my children (who were all grown and gone) each took turns spending the night with me. I don't know if they were afraid something would happened to me next, or if they thought I would be afraid to stay in the home alone, whatever the case they stayed. I've heard it said that your funeral should be a reflection of your life. William's funeral spoke well of his life. There were people at our house for the next week until his burial. I mean this house was full!! There was not parking spaces left on the street. At the funeral home there was a long line (including all the motorcyclists) waiting to view the body. The sign-in book was full and people had to sign in anywhere they could find a space. All the food!! I sent food home with every last one of them and I still had no room to put it all. I kept busy with arrangements and details. After several people spoke at his funeral we all headed for the grave yard. The reception to the grave yard was so long that the cars had to double and triple up to get in the cemetery. I was so proud of my children. They held up well and gave me the strength to follow through with his burial. It was only after the funeral when everyone finally went home and I was alone. (I told my children to go home. I'll be alright). I sat alone with my thoughts and said "Oh Lord, how do I go on from here?" This is the man I grew to be a woman with. The man I had raised our children with, my partner for the rest of my life (or so I thought). I cried some more (if I couldn't do anything but cry, that's what I did, cry). I knew all eyes were on me now. I couldn't and wouldn't let my children down, I had to stand strong for them. They called me ore came over every day. I talked to them extensively, I wanted to make sure on one was experiencing problems that might require professional help. They seem to be doing the same thing with me.

I thrusted myself into my work. Every time I tried to have a quiet, lazy, or slow day it wouldn't work. I would shake uncontrollably. If slowed down too much I had too much time to think. So I kept it moving. It was during this time that my manager decided to leave the bus terminal. I loved my job as a dispatcher but my new job as terminal supervisor was a bit overwhelming. It was like having 125 children who would all come to you and tell on one another. And every mistake made by these 125 people, the "buck would stop at me".

I loved the people I worked with but didn't want to necessary be responsible for all they did (or didn't do). Bottom line is this kept me plenty busy. I believe the Good Lord never gives you more than you can bare, I believe that I'm Blessed in the Mess and I surely believe I'm Blessed and highly favored. So I put forward my best effort to commit to this job fully. Good better, best, never let them rest, until your good is better and your better is best. I found myself thriving to make a living in the absence of my husband. Best help he could have left me was this house that we both bought and paid for cash.

I started cleaning out, putting up and packing away all my husband's things (this was at least three years after he passed). My two nieces helped (Toni and Chinney). William had plenty, plenty stuff. I made a mental note to myself to keep my material things simple so no one would have to get rid of my things like this because when you are gone you can't take it with you. "No one goes to heaven with a U-Haul behind them."

I started to focus on little 'projects' as I called them. I would work and every week I found something that I wanted to accomplish that was positive. I learned something about myself at this point. I never had 'extra money' before. I did now and I found that what made me happiest was to be able to share. I would see ladies in the grocery store and they couldn't pay for their grocery and started to put things back, I would say no take it I will pay for it. A church I knew filled a tractor-trailer up with goods, clothes, grocery and personals so that the pastor of the church could go with that truck to New Orleans to help the people there that were hurricane Katrina victims. This was a project I loved, because I trusted that pastor to do exactly what he said he would and I so badly wanted to help these people. I went to the grocery store several times trying to think of things that others didn't think of to pack in the boxes I sent to put in the truck. This was a way I knew I could help without my efforts going through unclean hands first. All the poor children and unfortunate people I saw on T.V., I hesitated to help because I felt that only a fraction of what is sent actually gets to the people who are in need. I had no desire to help the 'greedy' I wanted to help the 'needy'. I guess you can call me a 'cheerful giver'. I enjoy giving! It does my heart good!!!!! I have no desire to be rich, for that comes with a lot of added problems. I would love to live a life being able to pay my bills and share the extras with others. This warms my heart.

I spent a lot of money finishing this home, which was Williams' dream. He loved this project (fixing this house). I knew what he wanted to do, but he didn't have the money to do it with, so I finished what he started with his money. This pleased his children and family. They all knew how he felt about making this house a home.

I had been widowed about three and a half years now and I found myself becoming increasingly bitter. I watched other men and wondered why were they left here and my William had to die. I didn't see anything that they were so earth-shaking to make this a better world. At this point I felt a part of me died with William, I didn't think I could look at or think of another man romantically. Then I went to the funeral of a friend and saw an old boyfriend. I felt a tingle that let me know I was still alive. I knew nothing could come of our meeting (he is married) but it just felt good to realize I hadn't died inside with William.

I made a statement to one of my customer's husband one day and Alton's replay actually made a great difference in my life. I asked him why did my husband have to die and he and other men were still here, what were they doing to make this world a better place? His reply to me was let me ask you this, 'have you become a better person since your husband's death?' This was a very profound question for me. I felt he was turning the question back to me. He was saying his death was meant for 'you' to grow and become a better person. I said oh wow!!! I get it. I had become a better person without realizing it!

I tried to expand my world. I had been so busy doing nothing much extra except working and raising my children. Being a wife and mother pretty much summed up my life. What did I want to do now? I needed a new purpose, I needed a mission. I didn't want to just breath in and breath out, I wanted to 'shake up the ground in walked on'. I wanted to make a positive difference in my community. There were so many things I hadn't experienced in life. The one thing that William never let pass him by was the opportunity to try something new. It was almost as if he was in a hurry to make sure he got to experience as much life as possible. Did he know he would leave here early? Did he want to get it all in before going?? I don't know. I only know he got to live more life than most. He would try anything if given the opportunity. As I said before we were young when we got married, and we both grew up together, along with our children. Doing his time in the Army he had plenty tales to share about things he had done while out of the country during the war. And I could never understand why every year for Veteran's Day I would have off and he would go to work. I often asked him why he and other Veterans didn't push for November 11th off (with pay). If it's their day why would they go to work and everyone else get the day off. It never made sense to me. Does anyone out there have an answer for me???? Veterans of wars deserve that at the very least. I never tried to stop him from doing anything he wanted to, besides I don't think he would have adhered to my wishes. The one thing I was afraid of and had warned him about was that motorcycle, but still he rode. I think he was the right person for me to grow up with. He made me a "strong woman." He tested all my abilities, I would not fall short. I was stubborn, so when he wouldn't help me with something I 'rose to the occasion'. Still, I now had to find new goals and new horizons to chase after new challenges. I read a 'purpose filled life' to get some ideas, I joined the church and I made a pledge to improve my character, and moral standing little by little. Let's see what were some of the things I wanted to try? I had never rode a grain, never ridden a horse, never been bowling, never been on a cruise, never been out of this country and the list goes on and on.

My two nieces that were around me all the time and helped me pack and put away so many of William's things gave me plenty of reasons to worry a out their lives and their futures. Toni (as we called her) was the oldest of four girls, and Chinney, the youngest. Toni had two sons and Chinney didn't have any children. Two years after William died we found Toni dead in her apartment and she had been dead for two days. I never want to see that sight again, her body had deteriorated!! Chinney almost lost her mind, the reality of life and death had hit her hard. She called my sister, (her mother) daily to make sure she was alive and okay. She called me daily and if she didn't get an answer she became besides herself. My sister, Mary, decided to send her down south to stay a month with her other sister to see if this would calm her down. When she came back after a month she was somewhat better. Then suddenly, one year and two months after Toni died, Chinney died too, all she got to say before her death was that her head hurts and she was gone. My Lord what does all this death mean, I had to find some answers. Chinney was only 39 years old. There is something left, he has for us to do!!! I am trying to figure out just what that is.

Not This Day

I enjoyed my customers, interacting with them, listening to their woes, as well as gaining from their wisdom. I didn't think, however, that my exchanging advice with them was my greatness in life. I did think that my contact with the children had more promise. The children are our future, and we have some great minds that we can't afford to throw away (we can't let them go to waste). I was now the bus terminal's manager, as such I didn't get to come in contact with the children as much as I would have like to. I would personally go to a bus with a problem child and deal with the child one on one, these are some of the things I've learnt: The child is either afraid (there may be physical or mental abuse in the family) or the child is simply hungry, haven't eaten, and their pride won't let them tell you there's no food or anger. The child is born into a poor family and wonders why they were brought into this world under these conditions. I never ask the child to discuss their problem in front of others. If you do this you are forcing the child's hand. When confronted in front of their peers they feel forced to stand their ground, they can't afford to back down because the other children will make fun of them. I have a need to connect with the child. I have many ways to do this. I can take the child off the buss and offer him or her a ride to school in my personal car (which they seem to love since it's a 300) where we can talk privately, or I can give them my personal business card to call me later, or I can leave them with a profound thought and tell them to think about what I said, "There's no further talking from here to school, no talking, I'll say, just thinking"

I'll tell you her and now the phrase that seems to catch their attention most is when I say, I want you all to, lose that attitude and find an attitude, about making your first million dollars!!!

Now when I tell them this is where I want them to place their energy, Wow!! They get it. They are all smiles. I've hit on something that interests them. Who wouldn't want to focus on making a million dollars.

I learned another things about trying to help a child, you can not do this with others around.

I noticed one day on my route as a school bus driver that this young lady came to school every day without a coat. I had several extra coats, especially from my daughter. I brought the coat to the bus once day so glad that I could give it to someone in need. Major mistake!!!! I gave it to her in front of her peers and she threw it on the ground and ran to her class crying. Mental note: Never give a gift in front of others… They do not want their business out front like that!

Our youth today are in such peril. The amount of pressure and stress has to be almost unbearable. There's the desire to be popular, the pressure to join a gang, the fear of wearing the wrong clothes and the competitive conditions both in the classrooms and the athletic fields. Couple this with, violence, violence, violence. Seems there's no regard for taking a human life. One can easily say that when they took prayer out of the schools, the devil walked in. So many taking guns to school and killing our young people. I don't know how many studies are being done on this generation of children but I'm willing to bet that some of this had to do with 'crack babies' growing up. I believe that all those babies born with 'crack' in their systems are growing up, they have little or no conscious, little desire to separate right from wrong, and a ruthless will to get what they want at any cost. There's no telling what damage has been done to their brains. They had no choice in the matter, these drugs were put into their systems even before birth. Their parents had marked them with this curse before they even entered this world. Why would you do this to your child or any child??? And now they are unleashed into the world. This is also the generation of the "Burger King" children. They have to have it "their way". I really could not afford a child of this generation. I'm glad mine are grown and its my children's problem not to try and raise their kid. These children have to have I-pods, cell phones, computer games (that cost hundreds) sneakers and jeans that are name brands, that also cost hundreds, hair-dos and nails and toes done, lets not forget the false eyelashes and on and on...wow!!!

I had a point system with my children. You got food and clothes, and a warm place to sleep on me, free. I brought you in this world so I'm required to do that. After that anything extra you had to earn. I put an extra duty list on the wall every week. After my children did their regular chores if they wanted to earn extra money for something they had to do something extra from that list. It worked well in my household. My children were glad to do the extra's to get the extra money.

This generation has to have cosmetic surgeries to enlarge their breasts and decrease their waistlines, to brighten their teeth, enhance their lips and on and on. Their way... What happens to the poor child who's parents can barely keep a roof over their heads and clothes on their backs?

Rarely do I find a young person anymore that's willing to do it the old fashioned way. Work for it!!! If you see a young person working at McDonalds or Wendy's, or KFC they all have such miserable attitudes, you can tell they hate to be there. They want to get it the fast way. Selling drugs is attractive to them. They wear plenty Bling, Bling, (gold).

Thye have coined the phrase, "work smart, not hard". I wager to bet that in another 20 years you won't be able to find any young person that has put in over 20 years at any job. They will be saying 'what,' your mother worked the same job for 30 years!!! That's amazing!!! That's why we are running out of money in our Social Security system.

In my personal life I continued to keep busy with projects. I know William had a strong desire to make our house a decent home. We had brought it paying the total price in cash, using his and my 401k retirement funds from both our jobs. We applied for and got a loan to put a new roof and siding on the house. There were several things left to do to finish this house. I got busy hiring professionals to complete the work. I knew fully well how William wanted this home to look. He had talked all the time about what this house would look like once completed. I would not be able to sleep if I didn't do this. It was as if he was talking to me as I went along. These monies were afforded to me from his accidental death. I knew I needed to make good use of it. I didn't want his death to have been I vain. It took about two years to get everything done. Once finished I cried, it sadden me to see his dream come true and to know he didn't live to see it. You may think of me as strange but I would hear him walking around in here when I knew no one was home but me, I still hear him even to this day. No, it doesn't frighten me I believe he's very happy moving around in this home that's finally finished with his money.

I know William wouldn't harm me. I believe he's here to watch over things (including me). I could tell you some strange happenings that I know were caused by him, but I don't want to get too far in that direction. I'll just say he has helped me a lot. After the death of my nieces, the realization of how sudden life can end hit me hard. I went back over that phrase in my mind that by the time you are 50 half the people you know will be dead. And in my case how about half your family. Both my parents were dead, two of my siblings were dead, all my aunts and uncles (except one aunt) were dead, one of my children and my husband! I had one living sister left and one living brother. It was at this time that cousins started to reach out to me by way of the computer. I hadn't met any of my father's siblings children but they found me and my sister and invited us to a reunion in Georgia. It was nice. I never had a cousin before and on this day I met 11 of them, my father's sister children. Wow, I'm almost 60 and now I meet my cousins.

I went car hunting. I said to myself since tomorrow is not promised to anyone I think I will buy my dream car. I bought a Chrysler 300. I said I would drive it if I only lived a week to do so. Four years later I'm still driving it. I had only 94 miles on it when I brought it home. First brand new car I ever had. I had a nice home (paid for) a nice car and more money than I needed. This was my new, phrase 'I'm not rich, but I have more money than I need' so I shared, and I didn't forget his (our) children or his family. I have never considered myself to be a selfish person anyway. A lot of people looked at me in awe and said why don't you just put it I the bank, stop sharing all your money with everyone, but it seems the more I shared, the more my money "doubled" and I have a lot to my church. My main concern was to have my bills paid. I was never a very materialistic person, I enjoyed the simple things in life. I know to some it seemed I had it all. But I knew the truth, these 'things' couldn't fill the void in my life, they couldn't cover the hole in my heart. Every time I would try to slow down from working I would get the 'shakes' I had to stay busy. I didn't need the money I needed to stay occupied.

Well I had two good jobs, a nice home (small but nice) a nice car and emptiness inside of me that I had a need to try to fill. So I started now to challenge myself to reach other goals.

I have a lot of work to do on improving myself. I know I have a big heart (in fact I joke about his when the doctors said I had an enlarged heart a few years back) I know I have a willing spirit, and I know I try to help those in need. I'm a person that if I can't help you, I won't hurt you. But still I want to continue to become a better person. I encouraged all who I encountered in my daily life to do the same. 'Work on myself', strive to be a better person. I want to be a worthwhile person, a person who makes a difference. As young people say, 'Don't talk about it, be about it'. I don't want it said that I talked a good game but didn't live up to my conversation. In my family I think my nephews are in grave need of inspiration, their mothers were what I considered as 'needy' young women, they couldn't figure out how to get a 'toe-hold' in life. I hope my nieces have found peace in death. I would love to see the cycle end with these young men finding their greatness in life. All my nephews, because I have another one that has his 'demons' to fight for different reasons, and I'm praying he finds his peace while still on this earth. Every New Year resolutions would always be to make some improvement in my character and my physical health. Before William died he had brought me a pin-stripped black pants suit, for my 52 birthday. I pulled it out the closet and looked at the size. I promised the Good Lord if He let me live to see '50' that I would quit smoking. (My mother died at the age of 49). I quit and as a result, I gained weight.

One day William made the comment that I'll never get back in any of my old clothes again and that he had wasted his money on that pant suit (which still had the sale tags on it). I think I was 54 about this time. Well after his death (I was 55 when he died) I got to thinking about what he said. I decided to make my next project a goal to get back in that pant suit. So on my 58th birthday I wanted to wear that pant suit to work. To put more pressure on myself I told everyone at work that I intended to wear that suit on my birthday. I not only got encouragement but also got support of those who wanted to exercise and diet with me. We did a 'biggest weight loss program' at work for two months. I won the prizes!! I was so proud of myself and on my 58th year birthday I did wear that pant suit and I said out loud to William, "see you didn't waste your money after all". I was (and am) aware how I'm being watched, looked up to on my job and in my community, I take this role model business very serious. I can't afford to let these young impressionable people down. But I do tell them what they see or perceive to be the situation isn't necessarily the case and when they wish for something to be careful what they ask for. Wanting to won my 300 (car) would set them back a pretty penny when it came to car payments. I let them know that I drove plenty raggedy cars until my kids were grown and I could afford to make that kind of payment. But let me tell you this, 'a raggedy ride beats a pretty walk' any day. Do what you can when you can. You have to crawl before you can walk. Don't expect to be where I am at 60, when you are only 25. I assured them that I went through my trials and tribulations too.

Having met this goal I seeked to find my next project. I decided I would go back down 'South' for my 40th class reunion. I thought it would be fun to see all my old classmates and exchange stories and pictures of our lives over the last 40 years. It's always fund to see how well everyone had gotten through the aging process.

I left the last two days in July for my trip back to Florida. I had planned to drive the trip alone. I was challenging myself again. The ride was pretty uneventful, but pleasant. I drove at my own speed, stopped wherever and whenever I wanted to. I surprised myself in that I wasn't lonely or afraid. I had a lot of good music(Thanks to my D.J. son) and I had plenty time to just think and reflect. This was several years after the death of my husband and I wanted to take some inventory of myself. I had been doing Tae-Bo for the last three years and had become quite strong, and physically fit. I wondered how I compared to my classmates. Oh well, I would soon find out. I drove for about 10 hours, then I started to look for somewhere to stop and sleep for the night. I wouldn't chance driving at night, besides I didn't want to take the chance of getting sleepy behind the wheel. I would get a fresh start tomorrow. I found a motel and took a bath and went right to sleep. I got up early and decided that I was about half-way to my destination. I was right on the borderline between Virginia and North Carolina. I went to get some breakfast and decided to eat it at the restaurant. There were a few truckers who thought that my travelling alone such a long distance was wonderful. (they noticed the New York tag and I told them I was headed for Florida). I smiled to myself as I got back into my car. I said, out loud, 'I can do this'. I pulled into my hotel in Melbourne, Florida at 'dusk'. I checked in, took a bath and went to the 'fish fry' right by the school. I was so thrilled to see everyone and they seemed just as happy to see me. Almost everyone seemed to have done fairly well for themselves (especially since this was such a small community) at least eight of my classmates were teachers, one was a principal, two were councilmen, two were in the newspaper business. I was a little disappointed that my old boyfriend was unable to make it. He was the son of the principal of our high school. I learned that our principal had died and his son had moved to New Jersey. I enjoyed all those who had showed up. The next day we went shopping and site-seeing. The town had grown so and was very beautiful. That heat was getting to me, that's the one thing I didn't miss about the 'South'. I spent a very busy but rewarding day which began by all of us meeting at the lovely home of a classmate whose husband built and constructed the house. After breakfast at her home I got a little tour of the town, then shopping. That night the ball and dinner was at my hotel so I didn't have to drive anywhere. I dressed and went down to the ballroom. It was very nice. During all the events of the night I didn't realize I was being photoed and information taken concerning my life back up 'North'. I retired to my hotel room shortly after eating. I was invited to a private party in a hotel suite right above mine, but I declined. I didn't want anything to happen that I would regret later. I preferred to end it on a positive note. After I awakened the next day I made a decision to head home. Don't ask me why but all of a sudden I became afraid. What was I thinking coming 1400 miles all alone. Well I said to myself its time to head home!!!! I skipped the last day and packed up. I started for home and didn't feel comfortable until I was half the way back to New York. I made it home safely and a week later received a newspaper clipping from my class reunion that featured ma as the lone classmate that travelled the longest 'solo' trip to make the reunion. Wow!! Another mission accomplished. What would be my next challenge? I was still trying to improve on the person that I am. I still feel that the Good Lord has a plan and there's things he has in mind for us all to do.

Life was still filled with pitfalls and money woes as we all struggled in this economy. I have to say, 'I'm truly, truly BLESSED in the mess! I felt there was noting that I needed that I didn't already have, I'm talking materialistic. Although I was widowed, I felt my needs were all provided for. Is still worked two jobs. I am human so of course as the pain of losing my husband eased, the loneliness set in. I started writing this book in 1973. I actually wrote the first two pages and stopped. My life during the 80's and 90's were filled with raising my children and enjoying my grandchildren. As I said e before, from 1994 until 2004 those ten years were the times we (prepared all year) made our yearly trip to Mississippi to take care of William's brother.

I went back in my mind to see what challenges I had met. And what I would attempt to meet next. I exercise five times a week, I'd lost 35 pounds. (I was a Tae-Bo, black-belt) no such thing of course, if there was I would have been a black-belt. I did Tae-Bo for the last four years. I decided to attempt to finish my book. I have bitten off a heavy challenge this time, but its durable. I've never attempted anything that I didn't finish, so whether my book gets published or not, I will finish. Besides, I have too many people watching me, I have to set a good example. Its funny that I didn't get one single person to 'laugh' when I told them what I was attempting to do. In fact, just the opposite, I was given words of encouragement. And a lot of people felt I have a lot of knowledge to share and felt I should. At the point where I started to empty out my thoughts on paper on a regular basis, was where I stated to fear loss of brain cells. It was also at this point that I saw so many who were strong, vibrant, active people, all of a sudden fall in bad health. It seems to happen so quickly. One day I see them healthy, the next time I hardly recognize them. Life seems to turn on you so suddenly without much warning. This is why I told myself 'you need to finish this book now.' Empty out my thoughts before losing them. I try to write six to eight pages a week. I got serious in September 2008. I wrote steady until April

2009. I was running on all eight cylinders. Sometimes doubt would creep in and I questioned myself as to why I thought I could get a book published. Again, I would answer that I think I have something of value to say and in all my years people seem to listen. But most of all I hope that my words will make a difference in the life of someone who struggled to find their own 'greatness' in life, who had failed at living their life WELL. Live y our life WELL!!! You can't live anyone else's life. You can only live in your own space, do it well. I wish to live a quality life, not a quantity of life. If my mind leaves my body I hope to soon follow. I watch as I visit nursing home after nursing home and I wonder where did these people I knew to be so wise and full of life go off to. They sit and stare at the wall, a mere shell of themselves, all that knowledge, lost to them now, lost to the world. For those of us that took the time to listen, it behooves us to pass as much as we can on to others…in this world of computer answers, and no use of 'common sense'. Lack of communication. Texting and e-mails, no daily conversations!!! No one wants to have real conversations anymore. I began this book by saying "let's talk." I hope you are getting the 'jest' of what I'm trying to say. If I lost my mind to a sickness, I have shared what I could with the world while I still had a good portion of it. We have to get it 'right' in the end, but remember…First we must stumble.

Reaching For The Top Of My Ladder

I wrote every week in my book from September 2008 until April 2009. My children were still very involved and concern about my personal life. They probably wanted me to 'get' a life so they could stop worrying about me. They said all I did was work and watch t.v. or movies. This is when my daughter gave me her old laptop and my granddaughter put me on a few dating sites. I'm not a computer person but I soon learned how to correspond with different people on these different sites. I met a lot of different people. Some very interesting, some were just plain old nutty, some were needy, some were looking for a wife (to help them get into this country) some were lonely (like myself). It's true that this is where you meet your biggest liars. I did my homework and learned how to sort out the bad ones. There was no harm in talking everyday to my group of new friends.

I had been on the computer meeting people for about a year when I met and chatted with a man who lived in my same city. This was a first. All these other gentlemen were all from different towns and states. When I ran across his profile and it was my city, I hit him up to see if this was a real person. When he hit me back, he simply said,

I love your smile. We talked back and forth for a couple of weeks then I asked him for his telephone number so we could talk on the phone.

We had only been talking a week or so when he had a death in his family and said he had to leave town to go to the funeral. I offered to take him to the bus station. This would be our first face to face meeting. I was amazed when he gave me his address. He only lived four or five blocks from my house. I went to this address, and he came out with his suitcase, introduced me to his (grown) son and got into my car. He reminded me so much of my uncle Henry. I was glad to see he was a 'real' person. We talked as I drove him to the bus station and as he got out and gave me a hug and thanked me. He said he would call me everyday from Georgia, and he did. I told him I would pick him up from the station if he called me when he was half an hour from here. He did, I picked him up and we resumed our friendship. There were no instant bells going off for me at first. It was not love at first sight for me. But it was his charm, humbleness, old fashioned, gentleman character. He was definitely a gentleman and a spiritual man. He loved the Lord. They didn't come like this anymore, h is was a dying breed. I was drawn to his demeanor. He didn't drink liquor, he didn't smoke cigarettes, and he didn't curse, as a matter of fact, he never raised his voice or used any harsh words period!!!! I wouldn't have thought I would become involved with a man so totally different than what I was use to. I guess I've always been attracted to the 'rebel' type. One thing I cans say about my life with my now deceased husband, there was never a dull moment. I could tell there would be no drama with this relationship. I had decided that no drama would be fine with me, its probably what I needed at this stage of my life. So I kept saying to myself, PEACE BE STILL. This was the sole reason for the delay in getting back to my book. I was too busy finding happiness (again) and falling in love.

This man was so much different from my deceased husband, but I wouldn't have exchanged one for the other. William, my deceased husband had forced me to become the strong woman I am, and I needed to be strong to help raise our children and withstand all that life had thrown at me, so I thank him for that. On the other hand my new friend did nothing but spoil me.

This was a gentleman, a spiritual man. A man who simply loved to plant his garden and read his bible. As I got to learn more about my new found friend I was shocked. He had been born ten miles from my father in Georgia and knew some of my people in the area, including my father (who had been deceased six years now). I loved to hear the stories about the time spent together as a friend of my father. He remembered picking oranges with my father on a farm in Florida. He also remembered seeing me and my sister pull up with New York tags to visit my father in Florida. We moved my father to New York when his dementia got so bad. We had to later move him to a nursing home when he wouldn't stop smoking cigarettes and set himself on fire. He was burnt pretty bad. I was still working so unable to watch him twenty-four hours a day. It seems that my new friend worked at the nursing home where we placed my father. Daddy acknowledge him when he saw him mopping the floor and told my sister that he was an old friend he knew from Florida. "Small World" was my sister's response, but I never did come in contact with him during my visits to see my father. All my visits where made during the daytime and he was a 3-11 pm worker. I say all this to say were all around each other for years, but never made contact except on this computer site. We even discovered that at one point we lived on the same street (it was a short street) still we never made contact. I also discovered that he and my father had the same birthday. Every time I would become upset over something he would say, 'you remind me of your father when you do that'. I don't know but there was a connection between us when he would mention my father.

This relationship grew at whirlwind speed. All signs pointed to full speed ahead. I knew this was right. Friends and family, of course cautioned me to take it easy. They pointed out that I had too much to lose if this man wasn't pursuing me for the right reason. I threw *caution to the wind and forged forward full speed ahead. I would be turning sixty in a year and I felt we had not time to waste. He was diabetic and already sixty-three. I wanted to help care for him to keep him here with me as long and as much as possible. He owned his own home, he rented out one side and lived in the other side. We started making plans for him to move in with me. I helped him have a yard sale and clean up the apartment and put if up for rent. The last day in his apartment ad eh brought out the last of his things, he fell down the basement stairs. I'll never forget that days!!!! His son called to tell me he had fallen and that the ambulance was taking him to the hospital. In the emergency room after x-rays, the doctors came in and said 'you really took a terrible fall'.* He had broken seven ribs, broke his collarbone, broke his shoulder blade, collapsed a lung and had bleeding on the brain. He thinks he suffered a stroke!!! My fairy-tale world was given a shocking blow. I still had no doubt this was meant to be. He was in intensive care for a week. In extreme pain. I went to see him twice a day. He stayed in the hospital for three weeks. He fought so hard to make it back home to me, the nurses said I put them to shame because I came out everyday to bathe him and feed him breakfast, then came back to feed him dinner and get him ready for bed. I loved this man and I knew he loved me. I thought I would burst with happiness the day they allowed him to come home. It was a slow process but little by little he got better. I had to help him sit up in bed, then help him to the bathroom and I took walks with him everyday to strengthen his legs, lungs and heart. He was on the mend, and we were happy as long as we were together.

The phrase 'PEACE BE STILL' keeps coming to my mind. I was happy and content, I wanted the moment to last forever. I didn't know what the future held. I only knew I wanted to spend the rest of my days on earth with this man, this humble, spiritual, endearing man. Three weeks after coming home we went for Myles' first doctor's appointment. He was doing well. Two weeks later we went to a different doctor to check the progress on his ribs. Wow! His seven broken ribs were new healed. We were entering the holiday season and it was a romantic time of the year. We spent our first Thanksgiving together. I invited both is grown children and mine. We spent a nice day together having dinner and watching football on TV and just talking.

Christmas was fast approaching. Myles and I spent hours and hours talking about everything especially each other's families and childhood memories. So many similarities that we both were in awe. I would tease him and tell him he must have come from somewhere in my family's background. I could talk to him about anything and I was listening intently to his every word. Best friends, that's what we had become so quickly to each other. Best Friends, a bonus to a relationship. We talked long into the night sometimes about any and everything.

A few weeks before Christmas Myles asked me to marry him, of course I said yes. We started planning our wedding. He wanted a quiet very simple affair. I wanted a big party, so I could shout our love to the world. He wore his feelings on his sleeve and was very emotional, I knew he would cry at our wedding so I wanted to give him the privacy to do so (this made him even more endearing to me). So the compromise we made was a small wedding with his pastor (pastor Hunter) conducting and two of his church members as witnesses. He was a Deacon in a small church, and then the next day we would have a large reception. We had over two hundred people at the reception. Myles and I dressed in maroon and beige, matching outfits, everything went off well. I wrote to the dating site on the computer where we met and told them of our story. They wanted me to send pictures and tell our story. They later printed our story and made us one of their success stories of 2010 titled: "they are each other's best friend." I couldn't believe all of this was real. Our special love story was on the web-site for all to read about.

So you can understand the reason for the pause in my writing from the moment I met him, at that point my mind was just butter. I had no thoughts to write down. I woke up with him on my mind and went to bed with him on my mind and everything in between was us trying to out-do each other to who could do more for the other. I LOVED it!!! We went everywhere together, to the store for groceries, to church, long rides, planted flowers, then a vegetable garden, took trips to meet each other families, life was beautiful. After being married for six months, I slowly started to relax and realized our love would last as long as life lasted. I needed to get back to this book. I still wanted to scream, PEACE BE STILL!!! But I have to bring my head out of the clouds and get on with the business of being a productive adult in this real world.

Oh how I wish that it were possible for me to make my life stand still! Of course that is not possible and life goes on as usual. I knew this to be so when William (my first husband) died and nothing stopped. The bills went on, the laughter didn't stop, obligations still had to be fulfilled, that ole clock on the wall kept ticking away, minute by minute, day by day and week by week. Nothing stopped!!! I am reminded that as long as you are above ground and breathing you are not afforded the opportunity to do anything other than to keep putting down one foot in front of the other until you walk through to your tomorrows. Good, bad, ugly, you have to keep on going. What happens to those that fall by the way-side? They get trampled over as the others keep right o walking. You see, everybody dies, but not everyone lives. Just breathing in and out is not living, you are merely existing. Live 'your best life'. Its yours to live.

I stumbled in my life, gained knowledge mostly by experience and listening. Whether it was listening to older people, smarter people, or an experienced person in their craft. Communication to me was and is very important that's why I think a lot is lost when there is no face to face talking. Not being able to look into someone eyes to get a 'feel' for what that person is saying or get a sense of what he or she is trying to convey to you is at a loss. There's no real intimacy in a conversation through a computer. (I'm not talking about cyber-sex, I'm not talking about 'sex' period). I wonder if the older people of this world have paid attention over the last decade as to how the 'art of communication' has deteriorated. Scribbling cut-off word, texting (unfortunately probably, rush, rush, while driving) seems to be the most popular means of late. Then there's heavy metal, music that prompt our children to be self-destructive, or to glorify suicide. There's rap music which encourages fighting and 'gang-banging'. The language is both harsh and derogatory to their girlfriends, boyfriends, home-boys, baby-mothers, parents, teachers, police no one is left out!!! Everyone is shammed!! For what purpose?? When I was coming up the message was, 'love, caring and sharing, bridges over trouble waters, what the world needs now is love, love, love. So much hate and anger is coming out of the mouths of babies now. And its staring at a younger and younger age. They seem to be born angry. It would be nice to hear a conversation in public by two or more young people where they were actually discussing a subject of substance that there were no curse words being used, or drilling (belittling one another).

When was the last time you can remember young people in public saying a kind word to one another or even giving a compliment. They have to put up a front to prove they aren't soft.

Showing concern for one another or displaying kindness is a sign of weakness to the young people. Listening to the language that comes out of 'some' of their mouths makes my ears burn.

I've actually learned new (horrible) phrases from them, things I've never heard said before. (I bet they can't spell them). I say some of the children because I realize its not all. And there within lies the hope for our future. So much killing and death!! Its' definitely not easy to be a teenager in today's world. If I didn't already have grown children I would bring them into this world of today.

I still think that the key to getting a child to trust and open up to you is in displaying a 'caring heart.' A child is not easily fooled, you have to have compassion, warmth, and love to gain a line of communication. Giving them help on how to stay out of trouble, or knowledge on h ow to save money or skills on how they should study or background information on how Blessed they are as compared to years ago just does not work. Simply put!!!! A child doesn't' care how much you know until they know how much you care!!! I am baffled to hear how they talk to one another especially their friends. I guess the use of endearing words are a thing of the past. They refer to friends as 'my dog', or my 'nigger' even their lovers are now called my 'Boo' (this could easily be short for my 'Boo, Boo" a mistake) no more 'girlfriend', or my 'lady' is now my 'old-lady' or 'my baby mama'. They are so afraid to show love. I bet you'll never hear the 'Darling' every again (smile).

There's so much wisdom to be gained it we could just get them to listen. Who knows how long that wisdom will be retained by the older people. I'm sixty-one years old and over the years I've gained knowledge and wisdom from collective sources, I hope that by writing some of it down before losing it will be of help to someone. I started writing this book in 1973. I wrote the first page and the introduction. I went on to be a mother and wife (a full-time job) for the next two decades. There are so many people I admire for their wisdom, Angela M. (the poet) and Mr. Obama, our president are just two, but what knowledge will their brains be able to retain after years and years fighting the 'good fight', losing some battles and winning wars along the way. We all are tattered and torn when we come through the battles of life. How many of us will be reduced to a rocking chair in a room at a nursing home not knowing the day's date, our own name, or the names of our love ones. Where does all that knowledge disappear to?? I sure hope that those smart people have the foresight to write some of the wisdom down before it disappears. At my age I can feel my mind slipping, I hope that there's twenty more years left with a good mind but you never know, I do know this, I couldn't have finished this book in 1973 or even 1999. I think I learned my most important lessons starting in 2000, and I hope to keep building on the knowledge. I do a lot of 'people watching' is what I call it. I pay very close attention to people's attitudes. I can just about tell you everything about a person's mood, when they enter a room. I probably can't tell you what were wearing but I can tell you what frame of mind they were in. I call that 'people watching'. I do this with the children too. This helps me connect with people. If you are aware of their pain, their problems, their issues it opens the door for a line of communication. I guess another way of looking at it is, I find most of the time things or a person is not what they seem at first glance. I tend to look-over the obvious and look for the deeper meaning.

At this age I'm young enough to still enjoy doing things in life and old enough to appreciate the importance of living your life to the fullest. Living your best life. I've reached my personal best and I wish that life could stand still of course I know that's impossible, but now I have to find a way to share and give back to my community, to shade the ground that I walk on.

Keeping It all Together

It's so very obvious that time moves on, and for me it has done so very quickly. I can't believe its been a year since my marriage (March 12, will be a year). It has been for me a very happy, drama-free year, realizing that life can hand you a series of twists and turns at any moment I strive to avoid things, people or situations that could become problems Myles and I visited several different churches, including his church. We took long rides together and enjoyed gardening, very much. We lived a simple, but happy life. I had come to realize that I was enjoying my new husband and new lifestyle a little too much. Both my doctors told me to stop being so happy (this was in reference to my weight gain). I couldn't believe although I should have known at the rate I was going I would gain all the weight I had worked so hard at losing, back. Especially, when you have a husband that loves you 'just as you are', big, medium, or small. This extra weight started to effect my heart, my energy-level, and my ability to sleep. I had to get back to eating right and exercising. I was doing all I could to keep Myles healthy, cooking him heathy meals and making sure he took his medicine. He has diabetes. Each day we have together seemed extra precious to us both. I needed to get and keep myself in shape also. In the two years since I met him I had gained twenty-five pounds. I couldn't get in most of my clothes. I refused to buy any larger sizes that would be like admitting I'm not going to lose the weight.

I think back over my life and the journey I have traveled to this point and I Thank the Good Lord for the road traveled and the many, many, lessons learned. I wouldn't want to exchange nay of the hard times for better one. If I did that it would take away some of the character and appreciation I have built for having gone through these things. My strength was built out of these 'rough times' and I know today that I am a S-T-R-O-N-G Black Woman. I have kept many letters and cards over the years from young women admiring my strengths. I tell them all that life throws us all our fair share of rough spots. 'It's hard but its' fair!!! Every hard knock brings with it some form of wisdom. You should get 'something out of every hardship. Ad when you make it through another one you should reflect on what you have learned and rest-up for the next blow. It goes around on cycles. It's on you one minute and your best friend the next. Each wave of heart-aches brings with it enlightening skills as to how to best fight the battles of life. As a matter-of-fact, I'm rather proud of my 'battle scars'. You can tell that I fought the 'good fight'.

I've paid my dues in this life and I do not apologize for having made it to this point where I can say I live a comfortable lifestyle. I'm thankful for having good health, good children, a good man (that loves me unconditionally) good friends, good family, a good job, a nice home and a nice piece of transportation.

I will continue to fight the good fight, and my next battle is to get and keep this weight off. I believe I will always be on the heavy side, but not this heavy and much healthier. So I begin another mission to lose this extra weight (again and finally) as always I know

I'm being watched and it is for that reason I feel compelled to set a good example.

I don't want to be accused of talking the talk, but not walking the walk.

I began this book by stating I seem to have a 'gift for gab', I don't mean I talk a lot, I mean young people listen a lot to what I have to say. It took me years to realize they were listening. Children who use to frequent my house (visiting my children) grew up and would repeat to me one thing or another that I had once said to them that they never forgot. Most of the time I can remember saying it but not all the time. Even the children from by bus, once grown, would see me in the mall, or at the grocery store and they would also have tales for me of things they learned from me. This to me is and was very rewarding. The group I seem to be preaching mostly to now-a-day are young girls, young mothers. For some reason this year I have more young women drivers than usual. They see to be filled with much attitude, and a lot of drams. The attitude I know is coming fromm the fact that being young, struggling to raise a child alone, and not being 'free' to party like their peers angers them. Then the drams of having a 'boo' (or a baby daddy) and not a husband makes the situation seem further impossible. They need that 50% commitment from these children's father, and they should have it! I always tell them they can't give in or give up their children are looking to them for guidance and that they have to set good examples for them. Show your children the 'stuff' you are made of and they will try to mirror you. And most important they do not stay children long. They do grow up, fast, at which time you will be free again to enjoy your life, and be able to be proud of children you have raised. What comes out of these children is what you have put in them. You have to instill, values, morals, manners and help to build character. You have to lead by example. You have a very important mission to accomplish. These children didn't ask to be born!!!!! Finish what you started…I tell them believe it or not I was once young (smile). We all start out that way, I've had my share of the drams, hardships, heartaches and rough spots, but I'm a shining example of the fact that you do live through them and life goes on. They often tell me, 'easy for you to say,' your children are all grown, you have a nice job and a good husband and a home that's paid for. My answer, gives them something to think about. I let them know first of all I'm 61 years old. When I was their age I started working for this company as a matron on the school bus. I had three small children and a husband on drugs. I came to work every day, never missed a day. I had no car so most of the time I walked to work. I left this job and went immediately by bus to another job. After being a matron on the bus for two years I decided that I was as good or better driver than the ones I was riding with, so I went into training and became a bus driver. Thirteen years of driving bus ad one day I was helping out in the office because the dispatcher was out with a broken leg, my interactions on the radio with drivers was heard by the higher ups and I was asked to become a dispatcher. After five years of dispatching I was asked to take over as terminal manager after the manager left to run a larger branch. At this point my husband had died (but he had become drug free for 15 years before dying) and my children had all grown up, all of them had at least some college and my husband had even gone back to school and got a degree.

All if this has brought me to this age and this [point so it didn't happen for me overnight either. Simply put, I tell them when you reach my age you can be the same for even better situated than me. You have to live through the bad to get to the good.

I looked at last page I wrote in this book and the date was March

22, 2011. Looking at today's date I realize its been a year and four months since I've sat down to continue my life story. This brought to mind another thought, I wrote the first page to my story in 1971. I guess you can say I write as my life goes on. One thing I've learned you have to be inspired to be able to come up with deep thoughts and you have to have held on to your mind, and thoughts to be able to write them down. The mind of a writer has many 'pockets', departments, exits and trials. Sometimes we have to chase our minds, other times our minds chases us, and still again there are times when we are at a loss for any reasonable thoughts. This concerns me and I fear if I don't finish this book soon I might not have a rational thought left to share. I can feel the wear and tear to my mind and soul.

Let me update my life on paper since last I wrote in March of last year. I began to exercise ad eat right and lost 20 pounds. Myles had a family reunion the first week in August and I was anxious to take the road trip back to Florida and to finally meet his family. This trip would not take place however without a tragedy to this family. We received a call in the middle of the night, the first week in May. Myles, 35 year old son was shot and killed in Florida. Of course this was a very unbelievable, depressing and unthinkable thing to happen. What a tragic way for my husband's young son to have his life ended, so young. Very sad period in our life and we did what had to be done and buried his child. My husband being the kind of man he is was not only depressed for his son's life being taken, but it also depressed him that the two people charged in his murder were 20 and 21. They took a life and ruined theirs in the process, so young. So senseless.

We made it to the family reunion three months later anyway. We drove to Florida (Tampa) it did us good to get away and Myles loved being around so many of his family members. The whole trip was wonderful.

September came around and school began. My job and the stress of it really started to take its' toll on me. Myles started talking about retiring (and he should) he was turning 65 and is a diabetic, that job wasn't the easiest. Retiring stared to look good to me also. I had a bunch of new younger drivers this year, that kept a bunch of drama going on. I even had four different drivers and matrons that went out on maturity leave. That hadn't happened for many, many years.

Then there were the arguments, claiming this one or that one is "hating" on me (jealous of me).

My terminal is one third white, one third black and one third Hispanic. We've always worked together to get the job done. The mission being, get the children to and from school safely.

All of a sudden everyone is accusing the other of being prejudice.

I really started to look at my life, my job and my well-being. I had to admit to myself that I had become a 'dinosaur' in my job position. I held on to my caring, and sharing ways. I was still community-minded, and I had no ideal of how to be the ruthless, robotic, person this company expected of me. Of course I realized that business is business and this company was in the business of making money. Trouble is while they were analyzing their numbers and computer basing all their systems I was left working for and living in a community that I very much cared about and that certainly included the children we transported to and from school every day.

If I couldn't give 100 percent to my job I would not feel worthy. I started to look in two other areas that were quickly changing also. The ages of my drivers were shifting. The best ages being 40-60 years old. Those were the ages where mothers didn't need to have a babysitter for their children and the men weren't old enough to be retired. I had a lot of young mothers this year, who having small children had to loose a lot of time from work because of their responsibilities to those children who should, of course, come first. And at the other end of the problem were older men 70-80 years old who were retired but took up a second career as a bus driver. They seem to all want to work at times that was to their own convenience, often taking month long leave of absences in the winter months (usually going to Florida). Who was suppose to drive the children to and from school in their absence, especially since the number of drivers doing this was increasing and the numbers of my come-to-work every day drivers were decreasing. I have asked these drivers when is your enough, ENOUGH!!? What I simply meant was you were retired, children grown, homes paid for, money in the bank, no money worries why not just retire from all work and enjoy your families, and travel. Why hold-up a job that a younger person could certainly use. I'm losing my 40-50 year old people more and more and its taking its toll on us getting these children transported to and from school. I have good young drivers but the problem is those young mothers are out so often. I had for the first time this year four drivers/matrons out on maternity leave.

Another area of concern for me was in problem solving. I am a liaison between the driver, parent and the student. Ii find that 95% of the problems are a lack of communication. This year I'm running into more problems than ever with the parents stating they don't believe the driver/matron. Therefore it gets more involved where I have to pull cameras (all our buses now have cameras) and go through the films until we find the evidence for what the child is being accused of doing. This is time consuming. Plus with young people (my young drivers) there's always fighting about this one or that one hating on one another. It feels like I have to be everybody's mother. I need a break from this job where I have to be responsible for 150 grown people.

And finally, the Politics of this job does not become me. With me, 'What you see is what you get'!!! there's nothing phony about me.

I began to ponder seriously where my right fit would be at this stage of my life. I understood fully the scope of the problems with our children at this point. I also fully enjoyed my personal life which had become as drama-free and peaceful as possible. My husband is fully devoted to me and me to him. I'm thankful that my own children were grown and I am very pleased with their status in life, in fact my daughter and I had many discussions about the youth in today's society. I worked with children in the school bus transportation field and my daughter worked with trouble children as a probation officer. We often exchanged stories, horrible, stories that gave us much insight as to why these children are of the mind set they are. Good children are an endangered species. We need to be trying to save them just as we work to save endangered animals in the wild. I have come to believe that these children are the generation of the 'crack-babies' growing up. The product of parents using crack, and babies developing in wombs and blood-streams full of crack. We sometime refer to it as, over-cooked in the oven. Another way of saying the child's ability to think rational is damaged and impaired because of crack use, destroying brain cells. They seem to not have any regard, respect or value human life. This describes the problem, but what exactly is the solution. They have to start with wanting to do better first, to stop thinking its okay to exhibit 'ghetto-ism' (sagging pants, vile language, filthy surroundings) clean it up!!! Clean it all up. Gang-banding, getting high and not having any positive goals is not okay. Clean up your life!!!! Live your best life!!! Be an authentic Y-O-U.

It's not going to happen serendipitously. I need to know at this point how I could help. I have to believe there has to be a way to help,

I considered retiring seriously now. My personal life was fulfilling. I had good children, beautiful grandchildren and great-grandchildren, lots of death to the family of course but I still had one brother and one sister left whom I loved very much. We were cut from different cloth, but the one thing we had in common was a love for one another and a wish for each good health, peace and happiness. It does not make me right and them wrong, nor does it make them right and me wrong. It just makes us different. We choose our own paths to accomplish our goals. So now at 62 I feel blessed to be able to retire. My health isn't the best, but I have no more problems then any other 62 years old woman whose getting older. Either you get older or you get dead. Those are your choices! This definitely is the last chapter into my life. I feel good about how I have lived my life, and Blessed to have so many wonderful friends and loving family members. Looking back at my life I did all right for a poor Southern Black Girl. I have more years behind me than I have ahead.

Now I need to be able to continue to say I am doing my part to help make this world better I would like my grandchildren and my great grandchildren (all the grandchildren of the world) to live to see a better existence of peace and love.

My Final Charter

I began this book by stating 'lets talk'. Well I have poured my thought out to the world in these pages, in the hope of bringing better understanding, clarifying, and defining what is now the stat of this world (which includes 'my world') as it stands today. In my world I'm trying to exclude so much computer data and include more communication by good ole fashion conversation. The products of the computer age will definitely be lacing in the area of 'common sense.' A lot of which can be obtained by simply having conversation with your elders. I actually see families now-a-day texting each other from a different room in the same house. Whatever happened to going in the room and conversing? You have a good possibility of getting more than just an answer to your question, you might gain some wisdom. Computers and their data were definitely a large part of my job description and I will be the first to admit I was lacking in that area. My strengths were in 'problem solving' compassion, resolving conflicts. Caring and sharing kind of person.

I think it's time to retire from my position at work. Not to retire from life, people and my community. I still had a few good years in me where I could contribute more to my world than simply voting in elections and picking up paper form the street in front of my yard.

I want to help our youths, an assist our elderly. I have always loved to listen to the stories of the elderly and have gained a lot of wisdom from those stories. I feel the Youth of today are missing out by not taking the time to hear what grandmothers and grandfathers have to say. Valued information not being used!!! Information given by your Elders is given out of concern and with 'love' not from your computers. I feel this world is becoming to "Robotic."

The public can no longer hide their heads from the scope of the problems we have with bullying and disrespectful youth today. The video of Karen, the matron, being bullied by a group of children on her school bus went viral. A problem that we who work in the industry were well aware of for years. I got on the radio here and spoke about this problem as the fundraising for Karen grew higher and higher. In the end they raised over $700,000 dollars. Good for her, but even better for the rest of us still dealing with these youths, now everyone is aware of what we have to deal with on a weekly basis. May be we can get some much needed help.

Where-in Karen's bullying was bad, I could give you some stories that would bring you to tears as it has the child, the drive or matron that were being bullied. Lots and lots of stories.

He child or adult being bullied on these buses have several additional problems. Their hands are tied if they are the adult. The children have the rights and you have none. The parents tend not to believe you. (Their child can do no wrong) this is why cameras on school buses have become our best witness for bringing these problems to the attention of parents.

Even when you show these parents evidence that their child was disruptive they try to elude the problem by pointing out other problems they see on the camera of children that are not theirs. At one particular meeting instead of that parent acknowledging their child was punching another, she wanted to discuss the fact that another child was moving from seat to seat which I quickly told her that we would take care of at a later time with that child's parent, right now we are discussing what 'your child' did and we will discuss what others are doing with their parents. Another parent wanted to complain that the matron was hitting the seat to awake her child every day when the bus arrived at this child's house. The matron nor the drive are suppose to physically touch a child, so I asked her how is the matron going to wake that child. And secondly I asked what time is this child going to bed every night?

Cameras on the buss are not a cure-all for these problems and can be a double-edge sword. When you use them to show one particular problem, it (the camera) might expose another. Karen the matron who's video went viral was terrible but I can think of hundreds of cases o bullying that were just as bad some ever worse, having to take the matron or driver to the hospital. And if you breakdown in front of these children you really lose. That's the name of the gam to them, to make you cry. If you are the adult and you are made to cry in front of these children you will never, never be able to control that bus again. You might as well get a different school route (that is if you still want to be a matron or driver). You will be made fun of forever if you remain on this route. It's pretty much the same for a child that break-down from bullying. We have activated a program that has zero tolerance for the bullying of any child, still working on how to stop the bullying of the adults.

I was watching a television commercial today about getting the children ready to school and they were listing all the suppose available at all target Stores. They listed pencils, pens, paper, book-bags, etc. I smiled to myself with thoughts of "I wish someone could supply them (the children) with good attitudes". A simple smile can be infectious.

Give one, and you'll probably get one. They have so much anger. A lot of this anger is being transferred on to others.

As these children get off the bus at home you can get a sense of what and who they are going home to. You can't live in these conditions and not be effected by it.

These are children whose parents(s) are struggling to pay the rent, clothe and fee them, and often falling short. Battling to keep putting down one foot in front of the other. I watched the news today and see all kind of people challenging the elements, climbing mountains, swimming oceans, getting lost in woods, walking across Niagara Falls on ropes. Please tell me why, when the rest of us find it hard enough to just meet the everyday challenges why are you out looking for more problems. I will never understand this. Take small steps people, and keep putting down one foot in front of the other until you walk through your everyday trials and tribulations.

There's one positive thing about the technology of communication today and that is the massive amount of people you can reach in one setting. One can only hope that the right information can be given by the right people to do some great things. For an example bone marrow donations went up by the thousands when Robin on good Morning America shared with her listeners that she was in need of a donor, and the young men who lose their lives to street violence. More then half of them don't have life insurance (that include my husband's son). A 15 year old shot to death a couple of weeks ago, and of course everyone's heart goes out to the family, but who would think his life would be cut short at such a young age. A family that probably was trying to supply him with clothes and materials to start school with now has to come up with money for a funeral. Growing old is becoming a rare thing. The streets are taking our children. Using technology to express a need is definitely a good thing. If there's no life insurance it should be stated even if it's by friends or family, put that on face-book. I'm not a fan of these types of sites because I think they are used to tell a person's personal business, then to have that person get upset when there's talk about what was said. My question to you is why did you put it out there in the first place? You should use media in a productive matter.

Getting the word out quickly to the masses is the positive side of technology. The down side is the loss of personal (one-on-one) conversation. The exchange of thoughts, ideas, and opinions. They very thing that I have become good at (expressing my thoughts) has fallen to the way-side.

It's time for me to take my leave from work. I'll retire, I'm hoping that I won't take my leave from life. I have some friends who have done just that. They have retired from work and decided to stay closed off from the world, their homes have become their worlds, they are hermits. When I asked why they chose not to come out of their houses they say, 'why' look what's happening in our world. Shootings every day, robberies, there 's no more caring or sharing, so many evil people, and disrespectful children with vile mouths. Wow! What a horrible picture they paint, but I had to admit this was the truth. I had to ask myself where is my 'right' place in all of this. I really didn't want to shut myself off from the world. Such as it is, have I done all I can to help fix some of these problems? I believe if you're not part of the solution, you're part of the problem. I'm going to miss all my co-workers, and I loved being a liaison between the driver, parents, matrons and children. I have much love for the children whether as a bus driver or supervisor. I really want to find a way to help guide them to a happy, healthy, fulfilling life.

I've been blessed to live this long and to reach retirement age. I would love to live long enough to leave this 'ole world' a better place.

I would like to think that I 'shade the ground' I walk on. In other words, that I've help the people who I have come in contact with some kind of way.

I awoke this morning with thoughts of the entire world. Countries at war, children living in poverty, world hunger, global warming, just to name a few of our existing problems. I wonder how we can be lead to the right answers to these and other problems. We have a lot of smart people who are working on solutions and I have no doubt that computers will have a hand in helping to solve some of these problems. My thoughts go to Mr. Romney and President Obama and I am actually feeling sorrow the both of them. With all that' wrong with the world you would need big, big shoulders to bare all this. I look at how Mr. Obama's hair was become full of grey and I listen to Mrs. Romney defend her husband by asking the republicans to back off of him, stating that they had no ideal of what it's like to be the kind of 'fish bowl' they're living. I agree, I can only imagine the amount of scrutiny that goes along with this job. I wonder why anyone would wish for this position. Being the head of an entire Nation. I think the smartest thing that Mr. Obama did was to surround himself with really smart people, so as to have input from his people to help solve the overwhelming load of problems. Michelle Obama included as one of his advisors, I think she's very smart and has a lot of good knowledge to share. I can't wait for her book after the White House days are over. Not to say that Mr. Obama is lacking in 'smarts', but no one knows everything and I know that one person can't do it alone. I guess what I'm trying to say is I exist in much smaller world and I have a need to make my little corner of this world better. I struggle to wrap my mind around making better this community and here you have people (Mr. Romney and President Obama) running for office to run the whole country. It's amazing, almost frightening to me!!! I don't think anyone of us can come close to imagining the amount of STRESS associated with this position. My hat goes off to the both of them and their families.

I have retired and I'm missing the children, and my drivers, even the irate parents. One description that would never describe this career I have just left ad that is 'dull' or 'boring'. I hope these children and parents have learned some important lessons from their encounters over the years with me. I have certainly gained a lot of knowledge for having come in contact with them.

I had a conversation with a couple of students today that made me smile. They were getting off the buss from one of our new 'charter schools'. This particular one has a longer school year, uniforms (I love it) and longer days, school begins earlier each day and gets out later. I smiled because after my conversation with them, I was of the opinion that my future, this community's future has hope, they both spoke articulately and with respect.

I also found out that this was one of several new schools to our area, all of them going with longer days and starting the school year earlier and ending it later. Now I am just hoping these children can live through their teenage years in a city that has re-occurring violence every day, shootings and stabbings. Where are all these guns coming from!

Summing It All Up

What a wonderful world in which I'm Blessed to live! Every Black man or woman that have lived or were told about the struggles of our people should have big smiles on their faces today, and a beautiful song in their hearts. Only in America, land of the free and home of the brave, can a Black man become president again for the second time. There should be no excuses for anyone not have the faith, hope and courage to become the 'best' of yourself you can possibly be. To live your best life. I don't want to leave this life owing it anything and I don't want it (life) to owe me anything. I plan to make-up my 'Bucket-List' as soon as I finish this book. My brother told me a few days ago that everything I have started out to do I have finished. I had to think back over my life and I guess that's a true statement. It makes me smile. I was the only one blessed to walk the stage and graduate from high school. I completed and got my license to become a Realtor (I sold houses) I completed and got my license to do hair, and I kept all my children home with me until they all complete high school (I wouldn't give up on one of my sons, he stayed in 12th grade for five years) I stayed right on him and all of them have had some degree of college education.

I stayed with my husband for 35 years, until his death. I've worked all my life beginning at age 15 and worked several jobs at one time up until my retirement age. I now want to complete this book. I feel like I'm having my last conversation, the old fashion way, with the world. No texting for me, no face-book type of communication, but 'real' talk. My hope is that as long as I'm around (on this earth) there will be others like me who still like to sit around conversing and sharing WISDOM. It doesn't come with the correct answers you get from computers. The robotic state of the world that we are moving towards. Even telephone calls to inform you are being made my computers, surgeries are being done by computers, every form of work will be taken over soon by computers.

I feel Blessed for the lifestyle I'm able to lead today, I just miss so much good conversation. I live a comfortable life, I was never big on the material things, but I won't forget the struggles I went through and the mistakes I made along the way to get here. I Thank God for the road I traveled, the lessons learned and the wisdom gained along the way. This is what bothers me about our youth today. They're sitting somewhere all day with some form of computer (even when driving) texting their parents (who are right downstairs) instead of having good old fashion conversation. I remember my children asking plenty questions growing up like what are these made of, or where does these come from, who makes these, etc., etc. children don't ask questions like they use to they go straight to the computer for the 'short version' of the answer.

The get the answers without the wisdom. No Mother's Wit (like we use to call it) Good old fashion knowledge from parents and grandparents. A computer was of very little help in getting me to where I am today. I'm speaking in terms of my knowledge and strength from what I've come through. There were many, many, many hard times (again, I wouldn't want to change any of them) but I think the worst of times in my adulthood was 1985-1990. Our home was foreclosed on and we were forced to move in the worst of neighborhoods for three months until we could find better shelter. We slept on the living room floor of my girlfriend's home until this shabby apartment became available. All our belongings were parked outside of my friend's home on a U-Haul truck. When we were able to move into this apartment we only put the beds up and left everything else in boxes stacked in the hallway and in the living room. We had no phone and we struggled to save enough money to get an apartment. I worked at the beauty salon and my husband had a good job but he also had a drug habit. I do not wish to lay total blame for our situation on him I could have left him but didn't choose to do so. I shoulder my share of the blame by saying I choose to play lottery every day. While living in this apartment my youngest son came in contact with a child molester, who had been stalking this neighborhood in an old bus. He tried to entice the young boys to come in the bus where he gave them candy and money. Three young black boys became his prey. He liked young poor black boys with long hair and long eyelashes. This is what was stated in the newspaper. When he tried to molest my son, after giving him candy, my son ran out of that bus and told his father who immediately went to this bus to confront this man. The police made the arrest, he had a record and had served time before for this. My son was lucky, one of the other boys were not as lucky. He had suffered at this man's hand, my son got his father before this was done to him. My child was afraid for many, many years of strangers. The newspapers stated that this man preyed on poor boys in poor neighborhoods. This was the first time I can remember being called 'poor'. I started to take a good hard look at my life. I had to walk two miles to work every day and when there were dirty clothes to wash I would walk with my children each of us taking a bag to the laundromat. This bothered them they thought this was embarrassing for people to see them walking with bags of clothes. As I put my clothes on to prepare for work my last bra broke. Great!!! Now I had not bra. Yes, I had to admit we were poor. After three months we found an apartment in a better neighborhood and paid the rent and security deposit. We all were so glad to move. A few months after moving I started to notice roaches in the kitchen! We were not able to escape ghetto without bringing a piece of it with us! We lived here for one year then moved because of the crazy landlord who didn't think she had to give notice (she always displayed a gun) to come into your home and she did so at will. When we moved this time it was right behind a shopping plaza. I would take my clothes in two huge garbage bags and walk them over there alone bringing one bag at a time. My oldest son got a job at McDonalds and brought his first car, a four-speed. I drove it home from the dealer and taught him to drive it. I would use his car to get groceries once a week. My husband's drug use led to trouble and he was put in jail for several years. I got another job as a school bus driver and I was able to hold the fort down until he got out. I found the reason for this is people were much more willing to help a woman and children then they will if a man is around. In 1990, Mr. husband was released and came home got a job and we started working toward buying a house. Things got much better because my husband remained drug-free. We were able to buy that home ten years later. My children all grew up and moved out. My husband had missed their youth but made up by becoming a good grandfather. He went back to school and earned a degree in auto-mechanics and joined the church. He was killed in 2005 riding his motorcycle with friends. I've learned to live each day like it's your last because tomorrow is not promised to you. I've learned also that as time passes people grow to their own world. I don't take it personal anymore. I have nieces, nephews, grandchildren, sister, best friend that I don't see for years and haven't talked to for months on end because they are busy doing what they're comfortable doing. They have different set of interests. They are not to be moved from their comfort zones. As long as we come together when there's a need. I still have much love for them all and I believe that love is returned. I still love to give everyone 'love' a big hug and a plate of food. I love cooking, playing spades and conversing. So let's talk.

It's time to get back to my horse and finish my life story. Everyone has a story and this is mine. It's now 2019 and I don't want to get complacent about finishing my tasks. I have too many people that have shown me love, faith and admiration to let them down. I know who I am and I have to let it be shown.

A year ago today I was hospitalized with several problems including a heart attack. I'm still here thanks to the GOOD LORD. I also know the end is near. All the signs are there, you were promised 70, no more anything over that is extra. I turn 70 in 2020. The world has gone through a lot of changes from the time I entered this world. Technology has changed everything. I still like to converse but young people prefer to 'text'. They have very little interactions, talking. I feel like my father must have all his life. My father couldn't read or write. I give him the same respect as Oprah Winfrey gave her mother. I understood exactly what she meant when she said, Her mother did the best she could being a Black woman in Mississippi. I think my father did the best he could with his set of circumstances. I think this is my last opportunity to connect with someone that might have gone through similar struggles in life. My children are all grown and have set out to live their best lives.

I haven't seen or heard from my daughter in about two years.

Likewise the same for my sister. At first, I was depressed but I realized the BIBLE is fulfilling in itself. These are the last days. Is written, son against father, daughter against mother, sister against brother, etc., etc. when you mix that with this TRUMP era politics, this is the state of the world. Very, very different from my first memories living in this world.

My first memories were when I was four, father would go to work and leave me and my brother home alone. My older sister was in the first grade. He couldn't afford a babysitter and he gave me instructions that I followed to the latter. Four years old, I bet you couldn't find a four year old now a day that could do that. My mother was in jail for three years. I was four and my brother was three. He (my father) had very large hands and would struggle to braid me and my sister's hair. My father and mother separated for the final time when I was 12. This lead to me living back and forth from her to him. My older sister was out and married at 14 I think or 13, and my brother would live with my dad and I would live with my mom. Then my mother re-married and they moved very often. He followed the work. So when they moved to Key West I stayed behind in Hollywood with my Godmother and sister, Miss Jennie and Annie Pearl. I still call Annie Pearl to this day. Miss Jennie died some years ago. After living with them a year I went to Key West for a year. I went to live with Dad in Melbourne, Florida for a year, where I met and still are friends with Johnese. We moved in an apartment that we shared with two other girls. Johnese and I graduated in 1968, first intergraded class from Melbourne High (tomatoes, eggs, thrown at our buses and all). The night we graduated we got into my mother's car who had driven down for the graduation. My poor father missed it. He showed up as we were finishing. With a patch over his eye, he had gotten injured at work. He was heartbroken. Education was very important to him. He couldn't read or write.

I have my feet in one world and my head in to another. The world that I was so well adapted to all my life. The world that I became able to survive in comfortably and my head in the world of technology. It's now or never to finish this book that I begin well before these computers became the new sheriff in town. I still have to prove to myself and the people who have so graciously helped and supported me during my illness and down time. I have one son that saved my life. He physically moved in to help in my medical care and my eldest son brought me into the computer world which enabled me to become computer 'wise'. Thank you William and Bachi. To all my loyal friends (too many to call names it would take up the whole page). You know who you are and more important so do I. I'm today living in a world where I get to talk to my husbands' children and grandchildren weekly. They seem to still like hearing my stories. My children are all grown and gone, they are so 'over' this woman that loves to cook, play spades and talk so I try to be an inspiration for this generation to go out and live their 'best' life, there are some with good promises in this group. I hope to see them become wonderful inspiring adults. Me and my husband will live out a quiet humble life together. Out with talking, on with the texting and I drop the mike. (smile).

Haven swallowed big doses of life I feel that I'm reaching my fill. My body is showing signs that its wearing down. We burned my last living sister September 2019. There were four girls and one boy. My oldest sister died in 1968 after stating over and over she hated the fact that she would turn 40 in two years (she died at the age of 38). She was 16 years older than me, that's why you should be careful what you ask for. We had the same mother but different fathers. Her father was a white man and she was often mistaken for a white girl. In fact I was told that in the 50's on her way to the hospital in an ambulance they questioned her, found out she was black and called for a black ambulance to finish the transport. She left seven children in Atlanta, GA. My next sister to die was 14 years older than me. We also had different fathers. Her father however was black like my father. She died of breast cancer. She was a professional model in Miami, Florida. I won't drop names of some of the famous men she dated because everyone involved have passed away. But this sister that died a couple of months ago was very complicated. She once said to describe herself she said just put a question mark over her head. She was two years older than me and we had the same father and mother. I say to describe her better is to say she 'scrutinized' everything and everyone she became friends with. All her family members much follow her instructions and Bill her neighbor, travelling companion and best friend, tried hard to appease her but her often scrutinized (which simply meant, exam closely) everything he or anyone said or did. She was my sister and I loved her. We all did. She had two daughters left (two of her daughters died in 2007 and 2008). She left five grandsons and three granddaughters, lots and lots of great-grands. It was so hard on all of us as she lingered on in hospice. Bill her devoted friend carried out her last wishes.

I burned two more of my friends right after my sisters death. Margaret, a beautiful friend and former co-worker. She was given a heart transplant for her 70th birthday. She died at 77. Then my friend Lashonda passed away after along illness in a nursing home. She was only 48 and had seven children. Watching those children at her funeral just pulled at my heart. I did her hair for the funeral. That will, I hope be the last deceased person I do. I have done many, by request. I wish to only wear one of my wigs at my home going funeral. It's very hard to do someone's hair after death, even harder if you knew them.

I told my sister-in-law, Tina (my first husband's sister) that death is definitely on going at our age at least once a month someone we know are going home. Death is part of life. I see the signs of this world ending. Family feuds.

No more caring and sharing. I'm not so sure there isn't a big party going on, on the other side.

My husband has to have oxygen for the rest of his life, diabetes has definitely worn his body down. We live out our days quietly, peaceful and happy with a sign on our front door that says 'no drama zone'.

There's still me and my brother on the HEARD side of the family. He's in Florida. I hope to see him soon.

I end this book by saying I hope that I gave you something that will make you keep getting up after falling down. KEEP PUTTING ONE FOOT DOWN IN FRONT OF THE OTHER. Walk through the bad until you reach higher ground. Me? I'm still cooking, playing spades, talking to whomever listens.

I had no intentions of adding these two pages on to my book. That is until the year 2020 arrived. I don't know if I'll live out the year but I just had to write about how the whole world has changed since 2020 came in. The world as we know it will never be the same. I was depressed about this for a while, then I realized that while it may never be the same there's "good reason to believe that because of our smart young people the world will become a different but better place. As I have talked to young people and explained my plight as a poor black woman living in America they would often say, "I wouldn't take that or I can't accept being disrespected like that. They have convinced me that they have found another way. The year started with a PANDEMIC (a new strain of viruses) they called it Coronavirus/COVID-19. We were on lock-down and it hit New York the hardest. The elderly and people with existing medical issues had to stand 4 to 6 feet from one another. Because I fall in both categories, I don't know if I will live past it. Very few people have lived through more than one Pandemic since they come around once every one hundred years.

New language came along with the Pandemic. Words like "flattening the curve" meaning efforts to get the virus contained and "social distancing" meaning staying 4 to 6 feet from one another. The race was on trying to find a vaccine to cure this virus - Trial medication like Remdesivir or Hydroxychoroquine. There were no social events, period! No churches open. Everyone had to wear masks to protect each other from germs and Wear gloves and use hand sanitizer. Now in the midst of all this came the riots. There's been over 400 years of killings and lynching of black men/women, to name a few Emmett Till, Breonna Taylor, Eric Garner and George Floyd. These young black children are saying, Yes, enough is enough. They are putting the thing together. A smart child has many tools today. For information all they have to do is google to find the answers they are looking for. When you find a smart child they are really smart. There are some really dumb ones too, at least they are given the choice. To take the right road. I'm really proud of my children specially Laquanda who has decided to go back to college for another degree and becoming a shining example for her girls, she's showing them the right path and my friend Johnese's granddaughter getting accepted into SPELMAN COLLEGE IN ATLANTA. We may be getting old and tired but our children will take it on. **GOD BLESS THE YOUTH! TAKE THE BATON AND GO FORWARD!!**

I am very blessed to have lived through a Pandemic and a movement for racial equality over 400